You are not an artist

A candid guide to the business of being a designer

BY JON ROBINSON

Copyright © 2022 by Jon Robinson
All rights reserved
ISBN: 978-1-66786-317-7

First edition

Copyeditors: Time, patience, and friends
Proofreaders: Billy Frazier, Danny Harms,
Justine Robinson, Laura and Jacob White

Composed, designed, and indexed by the author

Printed and published in the U.S.A.
by BookBaby
7905 North Crescent Boulevard
Pennsauken, NJ 08110

Contents

Becoming the next design iteration of you

108

"Designers talk about creating a body of work, but they seldom talk about acquiring a body of knowledge. They take pride in being *makers*, but seldom identify themselves as *thinkers.*"

–William Drenttel, from "Culture is Not Always Popular"

Introduction

Why I wrote this book

Marshall McLuhan wrote, "We look at the present through a rear-view mirror. We march backwards into the future." That's a fancy philosopher's way of saying, "we reflect."[1]

After reflecting on two decades in design, I realized how poorly positioned the majority of design education and advice truly is. So I saw a need to get all these years of what I think, or know—or think I know—out of my head and onto paper. Mainly because I tend to have these same conversations about design with different people year after year.

I find myself repeating the same advice consistently. So what better way to avoid constant repetition than to say, instead, "have you read my book?"

---

1. Solid rear-view mirror connection.

Eh, that's a self-fulfilling answer.
Let me start over.

The real reason I wrote this book was the COVID-19 pandemic. Before it hit, I taught design for nearly a decade—as an adjunct professor at several universities. And continued to for a short time after. Like so many other educators, the COVID era had a significant impact on the way I taught, and where and when.

But it also changed my outlook on the state of design education and how I want to contribute to it in the future.

The necessity to keep people apart—that forced so many institutions to move to virtual learning formats—uncovered the most significant limitation of the virtual classroom: The ability to have valuable conversations in a shared environment.

When solely engaging with people through screens, it became harder to challenge perspectives, to collaborate, and to connect. Sometimes even, to feel human.

It seemed like the right time for evolution; to find a way to share insight and reignite valuable conversations about design and the reality of being a designer.

An opportunity to teach humans about this big, wonderful design world regardless of cultural, economic, or geographic boundaries.

Years of experience speaking, writing, and having conversations with people proved that I don't necessarily need a classroom to have a forum.

So, I resigned from my teaching job.[2] And here we are.

---

2. Literally, as I type this.

Who it's for

I've conducted lots of portfolio reviews with design students and emerging designers. I love meeting new people and talking about design. I can not say the same when it comes to discussing their work.

Why? Because too many of those portfolios are full of beautiful art and character illustrations, identity packages and campaigns for fictional companies, photography and lettering exercises, but very little actual design work.

It's not always the designer's fault. They just don't know the difference, because no one has taken the time to explain it to them.

So this book is dedicated to the designer who not only wants to be good at design, but wants to understand what that really means. Whether you're a student, five years into an agency job and still floundering to find confidence, ten years in and considering career reinvention, or feeling stale and burnt out from decades of poor collaboration and deadline fatigue, this can act as a companion throughout your journey.

Especially if you're navigating your design education alone.

But it's also for the design curious and the design adjacent. If you run a business or organization and want to deepen how you use design or design thinking to create results, improve the way you work with designers, or even approach leadership, this book is for you. If your loved one is a designer and you feel far removed from what they do, this resource will help you better understand their world. If you want to get better at working with clients, there's a lot of great advice here on building better relationships.

While this book may be written and marketed specifically to a design audience, that doesn't mean it *wasn't* written for a baker, or a financial advisor, or an entrepreneur. At its core, design is creative problem-solving, and there's an endless need for badass problem solvers well outside the confines of design.

So if you're a curious, analytical, strategic person who likes to break things down to understand them better; an individual who thrives on collaborating and solving problems with other people; or just someone who wants to feed themself with lots of different knowledge, then you'll find a lot of value here.

The information you'll find isn't just about what makes design good. It's about what makes design successful. That's knowledge that everyone can benefit from, as design touches all aspects of our everyday life. At the end of the day, we're always learning and trying to be better at whatever it is we do.

Designers never really leave design school.

I hope this will be valuable to everyone. If nothing else, I hope you can hand this book to a friend or family member and say, "this is why design matters."

How to use it

This book is a culmination of most of the mistakes I made in my career and the things I learned from those mistakes along the way. All the conversations I've had, be it with a student, a colleague, or a client partner. All the books I've read. All the talks I've given (or listened to). It's 20 years of teaching, and doing, and failing, and getting a little better at this design thing every step of the way.

It's broken into two parts. The first part is for everyone who said, "I wish I learned that in design school." It covers all the basic need-to-haves that are often missing from design education, formal or informal. All the stuff you shouldn't have to learn on-the-job, but don't necessarily need a traditional design school education to pick up.

And, yes, it's very heavily focused on shedding your identity as an artist and building the foundation for a nimble, strategic, problem-solving designer.

Part two is the icing-on-the-cake stuff that will take you to the "next level," as they say. It covers my career path through the agency world and how I transitioned to user experience design.

I talk about navigating freelancing and building client relationships. And there's a lot of advice on working with people; to build a greater level of appreciation and understanding of your teammates, clients, and other partners.[3]

But knowing all that, I'd like you to think of this book as a collection of conversations—focused on truths, advice, learnings, and mistakes—that cover the most common discussions I have with young designers. All the things I especially wish someone had shared with me when I was starting out.

I hope you can open to any page, spend a few minutes reading, and pick up something that will help you along your creative journey.

This experience should feel less like a typical design book and more like a series of 1-on-1 interactions. Consider each conversation your opportunity to think deeper, respond, and add your own thoughts.

---

3. Fair warning: I really nerd out in part two.

One more thing. I've worked with everyone from small startups to Fortune 50 organizations throughout my career. You'll not see me name any of them in this book. My goal isn't to wow you with stories of how I solved problems for Nike or cooked up an incredible ad campaign for Target, but to give you relatable advice that can help you tackle problems with your own clients, no matter how big or small they are.[4]

So let's jump in and figure this stuff out, together.

4. I've never worked for Nike or Target. Got ya.

PART ONE

All the things they don't teach you in design school

Today's technology makes it easier for anyone to be a designer, or at least call themselves one of any combination of titles: Graphic designer, art director, commercial artist, visual communicator. The list goes on. But design isn't just about making things look good. That's only a tiny part of it. A designer's job is to focus on meaning, and how it can be created and communicated. To understand how products are sold and marketed. To evaluate business problems and solve them with creative ideas and processes. Like the list of titles, this too goes on and on.

That's one of the great things about our profession: It's impossible to put us in boxes. As soon as we get a handle on all of the interconnected branches that make up the family tree of design careers, new ones start growing in all directions.

Thinking back, part one covers just about everything I wish I had known before I graduated from design school. If your professors aren't talking about these things in the classroom, you should ask about them and find a way to contribute to the evolution and articulation of these ideas with your peers.

But first, let's get a critical clarification out of the way.

You are not an artist

Design can't live on creative expression alone

I studied design in college, but I originally had my heart set on a career in broadcasting.

Growing up near St. Louis, people like Jack Buck and Bob Costas were just as much heroes, to me, as the athletes they covered. I wanted to do what they did, until I had an eye-opening conversation with my high school guidance counselor. In the I-know-the-real-world-better-than-you advice guidance counselors give, he said, "you're pretty good at art. Have you thought about art school?"

I likely responded, "yeah, you're probably right," and that was pretty much that.[5] Off to art school, I went.

---

5. It feels necessary to point out the irony of a guidance counselor pushing me *toward* art school.

When I got there, I was drawn to graphic design because I liked the sound of "computer art." It seemed new and different at the time. But during my four years of undergraduate design courses, no one took the opportunity to point out something pretty critical: What I was learning and practicing every day wasn't art.

I had to figure that out on my own.

This is a pretty common problem. The boundaries between art and design are confusing—*especially* for students—because people often talk about them in the same context. But as a relationship, art and design tend to have as much in common as other famous pairs like Marty and Doc Brown, Han and Chewy, Snoop Dogg and Martha Stewart. Hell, even Pabst Blue Ribbon and a Marlboro cigarette. The chemistry is there, but one is not so much like the other.

Understanding the differences between art and design is an essential first step for anyone in the early stages of their design education. But—so be it—many designers still like to consider themselves artists. If you're one of them, it's time for a harsh reality check:

You are *not* an artist.

Allow me to clarify: *Designers* are not artists. And viewing yourself as one—especially when approaching your journey as a student of design—is already a step in the wrong direction.[6] In fact, design schools share a tremendous amount of blame for this misconception.[7] I literally can't place enough emphasis on the responsibility your educators share in addressing this problem.

---

6. P.S. I'm not hating on art. I love art.
7. We'll get into that later.

Yes, design and art are very closely tied together. Many art forms—printmaking, for example—are undoubtedly the roots of our profession. And, of course, many designers are artists in their spare time.

So when you pick up that paintbrush, call yourself an artist or "creative genius" all you like. As long as you can separate that mentality when it's time to roll up your sleeves and tackle a design problem.

When I teach first-year students at the university level, this distinction between art and design is one of the first things I want to communicate to them. Like myself before, many of them are art students or have been progressing through a foundational education in the fine arts: Painting, drawing, art history, and often (for some reason) graphic design (the weird cousin of most fine arts programs).

While they do share many overlapping qualities, design and art are two fundamentally different disciplines. Each is informed by different data, is created through different processes, and wholly exists to fulfill different functions.

Most people who understand this believe there's a fine line between art and design when—in fact—there's a colossal gap between the two.

The differences between art and design

So, one of the first exercises I do with incoming design students is to explain these differences and break down the distinctions. For example: Art is about the artist, and design is about the audience (or the user). Art is subjective, while design is objective. Art expresses creativity while design leverages creativity. And so on.

A few years ago, after the first night of one of these introductory classes had wrapped, a student approached me and cautiously said:

"So you're telling me that this class is not focused on art? And I responded, "yeah, let's explore this idea a little further." To do that, I drew a two-column comparison matrix on the whiteboard, with art on one side and design on the other, and started to expand on the differences I had previously outlined.

Things like: Art has an intrinsic and independent value, while design has a value that's informed by external factors.[8] Art is about form, and design is about function. Art makes you think (or it's interpretive), whereas design should communicate and eliminate questions.[9] Art is about exploration, and design is about observation (and, if you're doing it right, iteration).

When you focus on individual motivations: Artists make art for themselves, but designers make things for other people. And artists depend on their audience for approval and praise, while designers rely on their audience to confirm understanding or usability.

The design process can't be based on intuition, or opinion, or creative expression on its own. Designers can undoubtedly make artistic choices to create compelling images, but, in reality, design is a humble "artform."

Well, that student dropped my class that night.[10]

If we were to really dig into the problem, we'd realize that many designers—and a vast majority of non-designers—don't clearly understand the purpose of design. Having spent many years translating design between different audiences, it still surprises me how many people on all sides don't grasp a designer's true role (or value).

---

8. Audience research, for example.
9. Design should be unanimous!
10. Maybe I tried too hard to convince her.

It's certainly not through lack of appreciation. Hell, it could be partly attributed to it. Non-designers are often very complimentary of design work, and are quick to give us the freedom to "make things pretty," incorrectly assuming that's our primary concern.

Early in your career, you may see that as respect. But over time, you'll likely have a visceral reaction when your work is called "pretty" or "beautiful." Or when you tell someone, in conversation, that you're a designer and they respond: "Oh, you're an artist!. You get to play on a computer and draw pictures."[11] Sigh.

The hard truth is that we, as designers, can't afford to make judgments based on our own sense of aesthetics. Design serves a very distinct role: It has to be functional. Graphic design, specifically, is the place where art, or image and text, come together to communicate. In my opinion, that's the root definition of what a print designer does.

Illustration is art. Of course, it is. But placing that illustration into a composition with text, color, etc.: That's where design begins.

Design is the business of solving problems

As a process, designers observe a specific situation or problem—or respond to a need—and address it with a solution.[12] Our job, first and foremost, is solving problems.

Typically, design (and the design process) should give order to an idea or goal. In an over-simplified way, design is really about making someone's life easier. Not happier, not more content. Not providing

---

11. Responses like this can feel condescending, so take them with a grain of salt.
12. With a lot of in-between.

more joy, necessarily, in the way art would. But about resolving an issue or improving someone's experience.

The goal of design is to support the function of content. No matter how beautiful or sexy the solution is, the result must be—at its most fundamental core—a successful resolution to a stated problem, answering all the questions that existed at the beginning. Any aesthetic beauty is a nice-to-have, not a need-to-have.

So design doesn't need to be flashy, it doesn't need to be ornate, it doesn't need to be eye-catching. A lot of people even argue that good design is often invisible.

We're here to deliver the most successful—not necessarily the best-looking—solutions. Now, you can be an artist in your free time. But in a business setting, you're a problem solver.

You're a designer.

Legendary designers like Paul Rand, Saul Bass, and Milton Glaser certainly injected many artistic ideals and concepts into their design work. And much of their work is appreciated today as art.[13] But we're also talking about artifacts from a time when design was in its infancy, and when the role of the commercial artist and designer was very much blurred.

Even Milton Glaser himself said, "design is the process of going from an existing condition to a preferred one. Now observe that there is no relationship to art."

On the flip side, consider that much of 19th-Century French painter Henri de Toulouse-Lautrec's body of "artwork" was primarily paid commercial advertising work. The same can be said of Ludwig Hohl-

---

13. And great examples, at that.

wein (known for early brand advertisements) or Jules Chéret (father of the modern poster). It's no surprise that this confusion between the two exists.

Design and creativity

Don't get me wrong; design is still creative work! The keyword that needs to be removed from the equation is "expression." Artists and the art world don't own creativity. They don't have a monopoly on it. Creativity just takes on a different role in the design process. A functional one that, when applied, can help solve a problem.

Designers and artists both work in creative mediums, and design absolutely can and should be creative. It's the "why" behind that creativity that matters most.

With art being a personal form of expression, creativity can come solely from within. But design is *almost always* informed by outside sources. We often have to educate clients on this understanding (or line of thinking). Right? Encouraging them to let go of their personal feelings or aesthetic inclinations in the work we produce with them.[14]

Good design isn't creative for creativity's sake. Creativity comes in the form of an approach to solving design problems.

Designers can, and should, bring creativity and personal experience into the design process in a way that enhances the functionality of a design. We should never be proud of a design (primarily) because it's beautiful or creatively different. We should be proud because it solves a problem to a high degree.

---

14. Notice how I didn't say "for them."

And, of course, a more aesthetically pleasing design will always stand out on the shelf and be more intrinsically attractive to a consumer. We all know that many people will buy something just because they think it looks cool. But if it doesn't work or solve a need, you can be damn sure they won't purchase it again.

In the end, consumers will always prefer a product that's functional *and* aesthetically pleasing over one that looks cool but isn't functional.[15] So designers must always put themselves in the user's or audience's shoes—rather than satisfy their own urges—to create successful, meaningful work.

---

15. Don Norman has a lot to say about this in his book *Emotional Design.*

You'll never get worse at design

As long as you keep practicing

We all need design heroes, so let me tell you about one of mine: A guy named Justin Ahrens, founder and principal of Chicagoland studio Rule29. While we've never run in the same professional circles, there's something that—outside of a shared profession—he and I have in common: We both studied design at the same small university in Central Illinois.[16]

When I was—to the best of my recollection—a Junior in college, he came to campus and gave a presentation to students in the design school. At the time, he was already successfully running his own agency. He would eventually join the national board of AIGA, author design books, and give talks on some of the biggest stages in the de-

---

16. And had the same design professor, Sherri McElroy, who gave me my first teaching opportunity. Thanks, Sherri.

sign world. But none of those accomplishments are related to why I look up to him.

What has forever stuck in my mind about his campus visit is that he didn't share any recent client work, and he didn't talk about any of his high-profile clients.

Instead, he showed us his student portfolio.

And it wasn't good. Or, at least, it didn't align with my understanding of successful, professional design. In fact, it wasn't any better than the work I had created up to that point.

That experience ended up being one of the most encouraging of my design education: Someone who had every right to show us up, instead, connecting with us by saying, "let's take a look at my student work and have a laugh at how bad it was."

You see, his goal wasn't to impress us, like most successful people returning to their alma mater would have probably attempted. He thought about where he came from, and wanted us to understand that he once sat in the same seats we were in. That we all started at the same place; the same level.

He knew exactly how to connect with us, and it was very reassuring.

The gap

When most of us are just getting started, we tend to look at other designers and put their work on a pedestal if we think it's great. We seek out design heroes, assuming they were born with a creative gift we lack, hoping to uncover their secrets. But, like anyone pursuing a new creative or technical endeavor, they probably started from scratch just like us (and we both sucked at it).

So if you find yourself failing early to produce quality work, I've got good news for you: You'll never get worse at design as long as you keep working at it. The key to success is putting in the work, every day honing your ability to perceive gaps and ways to improve your skillset.

Radio personality Ira Glass, host and producer of *This American Life*, spoke on this idea with a famous piece of advice on good taste and falling short that started: "Nobody tells this to people who are beginners, I wish someone told me."

Taken from a series of videos on storytelling, Glass argues that most of us who do creative work come to it because we have good taste. But at the beginning of that journey, there's a gap between our taste and our abilities. We're *trying* to do good work for the first couple of years, but it's not so easy to pull off. Or, as Glass puts it: "It has the ambition to be good, but it's not that good."

He continues: "Everybody I know who does interesting, creative work, they went through years where they had really good taste, and they could tell that what they were making wasn't as good as they wanted it to be. They knew it fell short. Everybody goes through that."

Sound familiar?

But you still have your taste. And your taste is good enough to tell you that you're not quite there yet, so a noticeable "gap" forms between the two. This early gap awareness often leads to doubting abilities— or a crushing case of imposter syndrome—and the people who don't know how to navigate it often quit.

If you weren't aware, almost everyone struggles with imposter syndrome—that inner doubt that makes you feel like a fraud—at many points in their career. I still do, as do most of my colleagues. Trust me: Anyone who tells you otherwise is either full of shit, or a complete narcissist. Imposter syndrome is a hurdle that can only be overcome by an awareness that it's probably not going anywhere.

Similarly, if you're just starting and already feel like you're stuck in "the gap," just know that it's normal, and there's an actionable way to cross it. As Glass puts it: "The most important thing you can do is do a lot of work. Do a huge volume of work. Put yourself on a deadline... It is only by going through a volume of work that you're going to catch up and close that gap. And the work you're making will be as good as your ambitions."

Put in the work

To those of you who feel you're already a master of your craft: The concept of "practice makes perfect" will always be applicable to help you extend your skills. I often have students come to me who are getting ready to graduate with a degree in graphic design, or young professionals who've been working in the design field for a few years, seeking advice on a common question: "How do I get into UX design?"

Most of them feel that their traditional print design education didn't adequately prepare them for—what they see to be—the next level. They don't understand how to translate the design principles they learned to another design field. My advice is always the same, and it won't surprise you: Practice.

If you want to design websites for a living, no one will hire you to do this if you've never designed a website. So design some, and don't worry if it's for a paying client or not.[17] But, first, look at how others have done it and deconstruct their solutions. Find commonalities. Put yourself in their shoes and see if you can figure out what they were thinking when making each design decision.

---

17. Seriously.

The goal is first to understand, and understanding comes from a wide range of sources. Once you understand how someone else used a grid, or why they made the typeface choice they did, you'll be able to apply this same line of thinking to your next project.

Think of it like this: You wouldn't read a single article on American politics and say to yourself, "I know exactly what side of the political spectrum I fall on." That would be a terrible idea, because your opinion wouldn't be very well-informed. A better approach would be to read many articles, from many different viewpoints, to form your own opinion based on various sources. That's called balanced research.

If you're not sure what good design is, then go look at a bunch of design. That's how people learn. Young designers often think that being a creative person means coming up with ideas in a vacuum. But ideas and inspiration don't just come to us out of nowhere. In reality, ideas come from what everyone else has done before. They're born from what we've seen, what we've read, what we've heard... what we've digested and remembered.

And it's ok to mimic the things you see, as long as you don't forget this is just practice to help you close the gap and get you to the point where you can concretely answer the question: Am I getting any better at this?[18]

Just like Justin Ahrens, I'm able to look at my student portfolio today and have a good laugh. But I'm also able to appreciate it as proof of the hard work I put in over my career. And every time I'm faced with a new gap, I know what I need to do to close it: Keep studying, keep practicing, and keep kicking imposter syndrome in the fucking teeth.

---

18. We'll get into more specific, practical detail on *how* to get better. Keep reading.

All designers start as copycats

It's easy to mimic a result, but you can't mimic creativity

The worst advice I received as a design student was from someone I thought I could trust. I was interviewing for an internship position with a guy who owned a small agency—one of the few in town at the time—and I thought, "this person is successful. He knows what he's talking about, and there's no reason he'd lead me astray."

His advice: Never look at other people's work.[19]

These were the days before Behance. Dribbble was a long way off. Aside from a few fledgling websites, we only had quarterly publications like *Print* magazine and *Communication Arts* (and other, various, printed material). He specifically told me to avoid these resources,

---

19. Bad advice. Did you happen to read the last chapter?

which were essentially all we had as a window to the lexicon of contemporary design.

In retrospect, I understand what he was getting at. He didn't want me to copy, intentionally or unintentionally. And, I want to believe, the emphasis was really on the latter. He was trying to prevent me from letting the work of others influence my own.

If I had followed his advice directly, there's no way I would have known what good design looked like. As my design career matured, I began to understand that an essential part of growing expertise is learning to see problems through the eyes of experts. And what better way to do that than by studying their work?

I read somewhere that "imitation is the sincerest form of flattery, but the laziest form of design."[20] But a little imitation here and there is certainly acceptable, especially when you're trying to close the gap between taste and skill. For a time. That's why I often encourage my students to first imitate, then separate.

Because copying isn't *really* a bad thing, as long as you're doing it for the purpose of learning. You just have to understand the line between inspiration and imitation.

So let's be clear: Regardless of what field you're in, you must be aware of the work your contemporaries are doing. Not so that you can chase trends or solve problems the *same way* other people are doing it, but simply to understand how others are solving *similar* problems.[21] If you want to be a designer, that means consuming lots of design media: Blogs, publications, podcasts, documentaries, whatever you can get

---

20. I can't remember who wrote this, but it certainly wasn't Oscar Wilde.
21. But knowing what the public taste is, and when it shifts, never hurts.

your hands on. Regardless of whether it leads to inspiration or not, it shouldn't feel like a burden.

You do want to be a designer, after all.

How we learn

The truth is: All designers start as copycats. All creative fields—like anything else—have a learning curve. And the typical instructor-led design education path tends to slow this learning curve down and keep it narrowly focused. But the actual speed of learning is really up to you.

Imitation has long been a critical learning tactic. Even Aristotle observed that it was human nature starting from childhood; to learn new things quickly by watching others and what's around us.[22] Today, psychologists refer to this as "imitative learning." It plays a necessary role in our cultural, social, and emotional development.

No one learns in a vacuum. Similar to our development as human beings, imitation plays a positive role in developing a foundational understanding of design by honing our visual perception skills. Imitation helps us translate taste to execution.

But it's also important to be aware of your history. Anytime you're faced with solving a problem, you need to know that you aren't alone. You should *want* to know how others have tackled that problem. That's why designers should take design history courses.[23] And why they should definitely look at the work of other designers.

---

22. He also said that knowledge is intrinsically worthwhile. That's a beautiful thought.
23. Studying design history also gives students a common language to talk about their work.

There's no need to burn time solving every design problem from scratch when you could be learning from the way other people solved similar problems. The process of analyzing someone else's work by asking yourself, "what was this person trying to do?" will only make it easier for you to answer: "What am I trying to do?"

We're more prone to imitate what we deem to be successful, so trying on other people's forms and styles is a great way to tackle the learning curve.[24]

When I was a kid, I desperately wanted to draw well. But a skilled drawing hand is a challenging practice for most children. So my mom would buy me tracing paper, and I'd copy artwork from comics or coloring books line for line. I technically didn't draw it, but it was an original piece of artwork in my young mind even though everyone (including me) knew it was just a copy.

And anyone who can relate to this practice should know: No matter how much you cherish those copies, eventually, you have to evolve beyond the copying phase.

Inactive versus active observation

You know what you like, but have you ever stopped to wonder why you like it? That's a big part of elevating your skills to the level of your taste: Moving beyond the identification of successful work and really *analyzing* it.

So what better way to learn how someone created something than copying it![25] How many times have you visited an art museum and

24. This is likely the closest thing we have to the master-apprentice model that dominated most learned professions well before the birth of design.
25. Aside from asking them.

noticed someone with an easel set up in front of a painting, copying it to match the style of the artist perfectly? Imitating the work of masters continues to be an essential principle of both Western and Eastern art theory.[26]

Even writers learn by dissecting the styles of other authors; authors that imitated the ones they admired before finding their own voice, reading and re-reading a novel before writing it in their own language.

By practicing active observation skills, you become more sensitive to what works and what doesn't. And an understanding of how to use simple structural things in your designs—layout ideas, typeface combinations, and so on—that you've seen work time and again can help lead to instant improvements in your work and help build your personal visual language. That comes in especially handy if you are developing these skills without access to university design programs or other instructor-led courses.

Just don't forget that you're copying to learn, so be very careful where you share that imitated work. It most likely won't be a fit for your portfolio. Remember, the goal of this practice is to influence future, original work. Not to spend your whole life at the easel copying others' styles.

When I was a design student, I wanted to be a digital illustrator for a time. To build those skills, I went back to that primary tactic of my youth with the tracing paper. I spent hours on my second-gen iMac tracing over the comic artwork of Darwyn Cooke, best known for writing and illustrating *DC: The New Frontier*.[27] I loved his style, which was influenced by 1950s advertising, and I wanted to understand how

---

26. It was good enough for van Gogh.
27. When Cooke passed away in 2016, DC issued a statement calling him "one of our medium's true innovators," while comparing his influential style to Joe Kubert and Jack Kirby.

to execute it the way he did. I'd scan in specific pages or frames that I liked, and I'd copy them stroke for stroke, color for color in Adobe Illustrator.

When I felt like I truly understood it, I knew it was time to move on. My style needed to be more than just a copy of his style.

Be inconsistent

A decade ago, type designer Erik Spiekermann was interviewed by Gestalten.tv for a piece called "Putting Back the Face into Typeface." During that interview, he shared his approach to designing a typeface inspired by another[28] as an exercise in "adding the sound" to letterforms.[29]

He said, "If I find something that I really like, I look at it for a long time. I draw it, and I sketch over it. And then I put it away. The next day I sit down, and I draw it from memory."

The result will inevitably be different. The new typeface will be influenced by the original, but not a copy. Spiekermann developed this method through years of practice by seeking to understand what has and hasn't worked throughout the history of type design.

First imitating to prepare, and then separating to execute.

Things like variety, diversity, and experimentation are essential parts of your education. I'm not saying that everything you make should be wholly different from the last. It's just important, as a designer,

---

28. This is common in typeface design, as many digital fonts are inspired by the letterforms of early mechanical type.
29. "A tune is a tune. But whether you play the tune on a banjo, or the piano... makes it sound different."

that you don't develop a visual style of your own, because every solution—and every client—deserves an individual approach.

So be inconsistent with the sources from which you draw inspiration. Be inconsistent with the way you copy things. Work toward finding inspiration and making it your own.

The process is the journey, as they say.

Find solace in the unfamiliar and push yourself to keep learning. The more diverse your inspirations, the less any one source will dominate your future creative choices.

The difference between imitation and plagiarism

In the 1980s, Barbara Kruger developed a visual style of tightly cropped black and white images paired with short, declarative words. Phrases like "I shop, therefore I am" emblazoned in white Futura Bold Oblique on a red rectangle.

The result was art—made to look like advertisements—questioning the relationship between consumption and identity. Her style was particular, born out of a previous life in advertising; the industry she was (at the time) reacting against.

For many, the name Barbara Kruger was synonymous with Futura Bold Oblique on a red rectangle until Shepard Fairey hit the streets with his Obey Giant experiment in the 90s.[30] While the latter enterprise has proved more enduring than the former, Shepherd Fairey eventually diversified and found a way to evolve that style into a

---

30. Or, in the same decade, when a boutique store called Supreme appropriated Futura Bold Oblique on a red rectangle for their brand. That's a different story.

modern-day empire that flows like water to wine and back again between the worlds of art and design.

There's no argument that his early work imitated Kruger, until he separated from her templated representation of language and image.

The Kruger/Fairey connection shows us there's a fine line between imitation (or even coincidence) and plagiarism. Picasso may have famously said, "good artists borrow, great artists steal." But this isn't art, and you're not an artist.[31]

Copying someone else's work and passing it off on your own—in the design world—isn't water you want to test. Many times I've had students turn in work that I knew wasn't their own, and a quick Google search often assured my suspicions. That's just stealing.

Your goal is to find the space between all the work you research. Experiment and probe the gaps. Keep at it until the work becomes your own, or you're able to put a spin on that inspiration that takes it in a new direction.

Treat copying as an exercise to find your voice, like Shepard Fairey. Or your way of adding the sound, like Erik Spiekermann. And, once you find it, maybe someone will copy you one day.

---

31. Remember?

Following fads is bad for business

Because trends are, well, trendy

A quick internet search will direct you to plenty of articles about current or future design trends. For UI designers, neumorphism is in, and skeuomorphism is out. Logo designers should expect to see a lot of simple geometry and variable type. Literally today, I just read that parallax effects and horizontal scrolling are going to make a comeback in web design trends, after falling out of favor in years prior.

And I don't care about any of these things.

Trends are constantly shifting. Every year brings a new list, and young or inexperienced designers are often eager to incorporate these trends into their work. Sometimes even clients are hungry to lean on them. They equate popularity as inherently "good for my brand" and tend to ask questions like, "shouldn't we use this particular style I see everywhere for *our* logo?"

Case in point: Several years ago, I developed a brand for a company based in the Netherlands. After a round or two of logo iterations, we received the most detailed and specific feedback—regarding the visual style of a logo—that I've ever received from a client. And it wasn't limited to a single style.

They built—and sent us—something like a 10-page Powerpoint deck filled with varying styles and specific examples of directions that they wanted us to explore with our next round of iterations. It was confusing as hell. Where did all of these wildly different ideas come from? How had they collected and researched all of them in such a short time?

We may have been divided by oceans, but not by design trends.

We quickly discovered they simply looked up that year's LogoLounge trend report and copied the top 10 trends—and the specific example they liked from each—and sent them to us to point out the gap between our work and what the "experts" were surely doing. It seemed perfectly logical to them: "Shouldn't we be trying these things?"

Why trends are a bad thing

If you follow design trends simply because you see them everywhere, your visual style isn't going to have a long shelf life. In reality, most design trends are trash. Like social media trends, most of them are nothing more than over-hyped clickbait.

More specifically, most design trends are inherently flawed due to their unknown lifespan. Like new cars, they lose half of their value the minute you drive them off the lot. If you intentionally design to incorporate things that come and go over time, your work will look outdated as soon as that trend is no longer trendy.[32]

By the time you discover something is on-trend, it's probably already at the tail-end of its lifecycle. So if you're planning to use a design trend, you're most likely too late to the game. Even the list I began this conversation with will surely be outdated by the time you read this. I hope you didn't waste time highlighting it.

It goes without mentioning that there's nothing creative or tactical about participating in these trends for the sake of trendiness.

If everyone followed trends, all businesses would look the same—all the time—and they'd have to rebrand frequently to keep up with the pace of changing tastes for trends. But no brand should look just like all the others. That's just not a wise business decision, which is why it was important for me to drive my partner in the Netherlands toward a design that was right for their particular brand. One that aligned with their business goals, rather than their search results.

In branding, consistency is essential. Consistency breeds familiarity and confidence.

A fad should never take precedence over a company's branding—or a product's marketing—efforts. And applying trends just undermines any credible work you should be doing throughout the design process.

Of course, looking at trends as inspiration can be helpful in understanding the market. After all, those trends were identified as such for a reason. They just shouldn't be your primary source of inspiration.

---

32. Plus, keeping up with the ongoing cycle of trends is tiresome.

Trust the process

Instead of following trends, use design thinking and research to create a unique visual style for each client that's ideal for helping them connect with their audience in the long run—something with real intent and purpose behind it. Every design decision has to be made for a reason, and backed up by something that informs it.

"Because it's popular" isn't a good reason.

I've seen this work in cases where design has gone explicitly against trends. For a time, in the health and wellness industry, every health food product used green to identify itself, because green equals healthy or natural. It got to the point where brands had to rely on varying shades of green to help differentiate themselves on the shelf, which only resulted in an overwhelming forest of products competing to look "healthier" than their competition.

And then someone, somewhere, decided to give the color orange a shot to help their brand stand out, leveraging the warm, happy, and more active associations of its brighter hues. This new direction was successful until it, too, became a trend everyone in the category began to follow.

I firmly believe that going against industry color trends is one the most intelligent things a company can do to say, "Look at us. We're different!" Or to help consumers find their way amongst all of the branding chaos.

I often use the rental car industry as an example. It almost seems like all the heads of the major rental car brands got together for a meeting, and they took a look at the color spectrum and divvied up which color each brand was going to own. Enterprise got green, Hertz got yellow, Avis got red, and so on. Aside from eliminating brand confusion amongst competitors, this color coding works beautifully for the customer, who only has to search for colors[33] amongst the other billboards and signs that litter their way to and from an airport.[34]

Now I'm sure this meeting never actually took place.[35] Instead, these decisions were born out of intelligent work that leveraged the fundamental design process.

So if you see a trend that you like, ask yourself: "Does using it align with my project goals? With my client's audience?" And secondarily, "will it make all of my hard work appear dated in 5 or 10 years?"

Just trust the design process, and be careful about integrating trends without very careful consideration. The last thing you want to do is attach your client to the latest fad.

Anyone quick to jump on social media trends—like the newest Instagram or TikTok fad—is apt to learn that these trends are often over just as quickly as they begin, and sometimes lead to unfortunate consequences. The same approach with design will ensure that your work is outdated as soon as the next hot thing emerges.

---

33. Not text or logos.
34. Often located along busy interstates.
35. But that would make for a pretty cool case study.

The problem with design school

And what we can do about it

We work in a profession based on the foundations of visual communication. And while those building blocks remain sturdy, how and where we communicate constantly evolves.

Each day brings new challenges for interpreting cultural, historical, and societal messages to effectively create meaning with our work. So we have to constantly seek knowledge from multiple disciplines to communicate successfully.

In recent decades we've witnessed a rise in the academic field of Visual Culture—the study of culture expressed in images—along with an emphasis on multidisciplinary education, but the connections between those efforts and how they support one another sure as hell haven't materialized in the majority of design courses.

Design education—like many academic fields—has been resistant to change for too long.[36] And let's be honest: Most college course catalogs are bullshit. They all promise to turn you into a fully-prepared professional designer.

If that were true, I wouldn't be writing this book.

In an unfortunate way, most design programs are like families: They tend to pass on the same values year after year, generation after generation, focusing on the same teaching models and assignments. Projects often discourage a deeper level of thinking that embraces asking questions about the purpose of the exercise. Are these problems worth solving in the first place, or are students just focused on passing a class?[37]

If you're now studying—or previously studied—design in college, I'd wager it is/was a traditional print design-focused curriculum, likely embedded as the step-child to a more extensive fine arts program. Because, let's face it, that's how most design programs continue to operate today, with little to no intent to change.

Step foot on any college campus, and you're likely to find a program that strictly adheres to that same approach, or one that (even worse) treats design as a trade.

Design as art

Programs heavily embedded in a fine arts curriculum stress creativity, but barely focus on the technical skills needed to generate well-executed and thoughtful solutions. As a student, you spend your time

---

36. Think about how difficult it is to find undergrad programs focused on user experience design education.
37. This point can easily be argued about the majority of higher education programs.

in typography courses learning the history of mechanical type and creating beautiful type-based layouts. Still, you don't know how to kern letter spaces or set indents without using the Tab key.

You can probably explain the difference between a typeface and a font (like it really matters), but often struggle to identify the appropriate software to build a particular layout. Any idea what a design system is? Probably not. These are things you'll assumably learn on the job rather than in the classroom.

These programs solely focus on the idea, treating design as another means of creative expression. Students graduate with conceptual art direction skills, but don't know how to color correct photos for printing. They may learn what CMYK stands for but don't know why the color separation exists, and likely have never seen a printing press at work. You get the idea.

In reality, this school of thought undermines the essential technical skills designers need *to execute* creative concepts. It leads to a general misunderstanding that the computer is somehow magic, and designers are the creative magicians that pull perfect specimen rabbits out of them by simply following a creative process.

Design as a trade

Graphic design began as a trade activity, closely connected to the emergence of mass communication.[38] Unfortunately, that's how many design programs are still structured today—as vocational programs inspired by the Bauhaus model[39]—further reinforcing the

38. This emergence of mass communication can be attributed to the Industrial Revolution and the birth of a new industry called "advertising."
39. A pedagogical craftsmanship approach that focused on the productivity of design.

public misconception that design is little more than a technical skill based on knowledge of varied software.

This perception is driven further by the abundance of design software available to the public, which supports an anyone-can-do-it attitude toward our field that spawned, what I like to call, Piano Mover Syndrome: "Let's try it over here. Now let's see what it looks like over there..."

A solid education that prepares designers to enter the workforce with technical knowledge, confidence, and expertise in connecting problems to solutions is necessary to convince clients that we're more than mere "desktop publishers," but instead authorities in our field. Like any other profession, we must strive to become well-rounded experts at what we do.

If you follow (or find yourself participating in) either model—design as a trade or design as an art—it will lead to the same conclusion: Traditional programs are not adequately preparing students to enter the workforce.

To communicate competently in our changing society, we need to equip ourselves with a broader view of knowledge *outside* the realm of design. A multidisciplinary approach to learning so that thought processes can better support execution.

Design as analytical problem solving

Connecting the separate focuses (creativity and technical skill) isn't necessarily the answer.

The people who teach design—and develop design programs—need to train students to seek internal *and* external skills, processes, and knowledge for application within the creative methodology.

Placing a greater emphasis on analytical problem-solving is how we make it happen.

I say it's time to reject both the trade school *and* art school mentalities in favor of design thinking: A process that, at its core, is human-centered and driven by insights.[40] An approach that pulls from many fields of study to focus on understanding and solving problems, not creatively unique or pixel-perfect designs.

Design educators should develop courses that challenge students to reflect deeply on the discipline and connect design to its culture. Students should understand how design has shaped the history of our society, and discover how it has (and can) improve the lives of the people who interact with it.

Great designers need to know a lot about many things; most of which will come after they leave the classroom. I'm talking about insight we can only gain by studying concepts that originated *outside* our discipline—like psychology, writing, and other humanities. For a typical design student, that means more classes, more debt, and more sleepless nights. It shouldn't.

It's really simple: Designers need more than design skills.

Several scholars have advocated for multidisciplinary design education for decades, particularly a liberal arts model. Because fields like cognitive psychology, sociology, and other social sciences can provide just as much insight into our work as design history courses. Leaning on design thinking methodology is a great place to start.

As Gunnar Swanson wrote in "Graphic Design Education as a Liberal Art" from *Design Issues,* "although each branch of study may be an

40. For all things design thinking I recommend checking out IDEO at ideo.com.

end in itself, the progress of each field of study is doubly validated as it contributes to general knowledge." More skills equals more *skilled*. When you combine a strong aptitude and knowledge of design with a well-rounded education in other fields, you become a more innovative, flexible, collaborative, and *employable* designer.

When these strategies aren't present in the design classroom, students often fail to see how to apply knowledge gained from other fields of study to solve design-related problems. As a result, designers often don't understand when they are ineffectively communicating through their work, or how a solution fits into the larger context of society—often resulting in an inappropriate and ineffective visual narrative.

Newly-minted designers then enter the workforce with little more than a portfolio of class projects. That missing contextual level—coupled with a non-understanding of articulating design decisions—can lead to lost job opportunities (during the interview process) or failure to meet or communicate client needs (in a professional setting).

Creative problem-solving pulls from many fields of study; many bodies of knowledge

In his book *Teaching Graphic Design,* journalist and design critic Steven Heller proposed that design programs should give students the tools they need to "decipher the various and often conflicting trends in our culture." When educators stress the integral role historical, social, economic, and political issues play in the design practice, students can understand how those issues impact how we think about—and approach—design solutions.

I'm pretty sure this isn't happening in your design classroom.

In comparison, look at any account of visual design history, and you'll see designers both reacting to—and shaping public perceptions through—well, all of those things.

Those who avoided the war between lecture time and nap time know that you can't learn design history by simply studying the history of design. You have to view each designer's work, movement, or style through a lens of its time's political, cultural, and social landscape.

Of course, basic technical skills are still necessary. The goal should be to supplement these skills with other learning elements that contribute to forming a liberally-educated professional designer.

Another way to make this happen: Educators need to seek the advice of practicing designers and thought leaders—across agency, corporate, and tech environments—regarding what they should emphasize, expand, or eliminate from the classroom.[41] Even Hannes Meyer, who became director of the Bauhaus after Walter Gropius, brought in experts from various disciplines to speak to students.

Instead of following the old design education model, new practice conditions must be anticipated and instructed. Because design provides strong connective links to other fields, and vice versa.

Identifying—and acting on—these connective links leads to simplified and more thoughtful solutions.

Many institutions pride themselves on the availability of diverse course selections and student requirements. Still, there's little encouragement from design professors to incorporate outside knowledge in the design process.

---

41. And we are eager to advise and listen.

So students receive lots of dots but little advice or encouragment on connecting all of them.

As the world becomes more diverse, those who teach design will need to address these integration methods. And anyone wishing to be successful in the field must seek them out.

We have to work towards a liberal, multifaceted, and strategic formula for design education to connect subjects and people across disciplines.[42] It's bound to only enhance students' expertise and experience, so that the future—and future designers—of our industry can thrive.[43]

But, as we'll soon discuss, the actual pace and space of your education are up to you.

Suppose we can refocus on developing broadly-educated design professionals who think strategically and solve problems by connecting to many disciplines; designers who crave learning about new things and applying those learnings to real-world problems. In that world, we will only elevate the level of our practice in the public eye as an army of thinkers, rather than makers.

---

42. Educators need to find ways to supplement technical skills training *as well*.
43. Also, broadly-educated people are flat out good for society.

Self-education is a sound investment

Success in any industry requires a robust curiosity

If I happen to find myself on your operating table, or at the mercy of your defense in a courtroom, I'm going to expect that you went to college *specifically* to do those things. And the better the school, the better I'm probably going to feel about it.

But if I'm interviewing you for a design position, I'm less concerned with where that diploma came from—where that learning took place—or if it represents a BA, BS, BFA, or WTF. We aren't making life or death decisions in this profession.

Don't get me wrong: A good education is still a must.

Design is all I've ever done, and all I really wanted to do since I took my first design course. But I was only formally trained as a print designer. Since then, my career has been varied, following a path that's taken me in several different directions. I've worked in everything from human-centered, agile product design to customer experience design to service design.[44]

And I didn't study any of these particular capabilities in a classroom.

But I've continued to train my eye and my brain throughout my career, to the point where I can lean into those things and extend myself to pick up new skills.

I often tell my students that when someone asks me, today, to design a logo, or consumer packaging, or even a website, I don't get excited about it like I used to. I've been there, done that. But the day I get an email that says, "can you design a chair for me?" will be the day I emphatically state: "Hell yes, I can!"

Why? Because it's something new. It's a challenge. And I'm confident in my ability to apply the skills I have, and pick up the ones I need, to give it a good go.[45]

Learning in the age of information

No matter when you are reading this, you are living at the height of the Information Age. Think about that. You can find anything you want to know with a quick Google search, and an immeasurable amount of information is available to you at all times.[46] Information such as: How to write solid SEO for a website, how to create screen transition animations for an app, and probably even how to design a sleek-ass chair.

---

44. I cover these concepts more in-depth in part 2.
45. I also see it as a great opportunity to learn!
46. In *A Brief History of Time* Stephen Hawking reasoned that "in Newton's time it was possible for an educated person to have a grasp on the whole of human knowledge." Holy shit.

I hate to burst your bubble—especially if you just wrote a fat check to a university—but there's so much design knowledge that can just as easily be found online as it can in a classroom. A quick search for a tutorial topic on YouTube will return hundreds of results, showcasing varied opinions and approaches.[47] Educational platforms like Skillshare and LinkedIn Learning offer thousands of deep-dive courses into specialized topics, and at a much more affordable price than the typical college tuition.

It's probably safe to say there's an e-learning course for everything.[48] And, in my opinion, design educators should be leaning on those resources (even outside of the classroom) to supplement coursework. That way, they can spend more time with students developing analytical problem-solving skills, and spend less time focused on technology.[49] Because if you haven't figured it out by now: Photoshop skills do not equal design skills.

But it's not logical to rely on the Internet as your only source of design knowledge. Hanging out on Dribbble all day isn't going to give you the skills you need to make it or the tools to help grow your career in a valuable way.

There's a fragile line between the things you have to be taught, and the things you can just as quickly learn on your own.

---

47. This is also a huge advantage if you're just starting your design journey. There's a good chance that you don't remember a time before YouTube.
48. You should also live on a healthy diet of books. There's no way I will ever make it through my Amazon wish list, but I'm trying.
49. And don't even get me started on designing business cards as a course project. If your professor tells you to design a business card, ask them if you should throw it in the trash before or after it's finished.

Design school is only a starting point

Now I know we just spent time discussing all the flaws of design school, but if you know—for a fact—that you want to pursue a career in design, then you should 100% go to design school. Period. As long as you can afford it. That way, you'll receive fundamental hands-on training and start to build a portfolio—the necessities if you want a foot in the door.

Design school will push you out of your comfort zone to try new things and help you build an understanding of what you like and don't like; what works and doesn't work. More importantly, you'll learn how to work with other people and start to build a network. And, hopefully, you'll learn how to manage deadlines.

Your design school of choice should provide you with an excellent overview of design history. Knowing what people have done, what they're doing now, and what they're referencing is a considerable step toward building an understanding of design. If you plan to break the rules one day, you at least need to know what they are and why they exist.

In my opinion, instructor-led education is precious. Educators should help you hone your mind and teach you how to approach problems. However, any school is only capable of equipping you with the basics, skill-wise, before sending you out into the real world. It's on you to continue building those skills once you get there.

Good teachers may inspire you, but they should also encourage you to learn independently. And it also helps to have excellent coaches and sponsors who are willing to give you access to what they've learned over their careers.

Ultimately, suppose you regard learning solely as a passive process that relies on transferring knowledge from teacher to student. In that case, it's unlikely that you'll continue important learning habits after you leave school.[50] Newton said, "An object at rest tends to stay at rest." So the path to new knowledge often starts with you getting your ass off the couch and seeking it out.

Adopt a learner mindset

The truth is, many people come to all of these things naturally. Some are better at learning by doing, researching, and observing independently. These are the people who can be their own mentors; their own professors.

As the Wu-Tang Clan's RZA famously said, "Whether I went to school or not, I would always study." If this sounds like you, you're probably already on the path to evolving your skills and knowledge about design (and other things) on your own time, without the need for encouragement or direction.

So, as much as I am "pro design school," I'm even more "pro-education." I believe that everyone needs to constantly feed their brains and strive to learn new things, regardless of profession or personal interests. And luckily, today, the majority of self-directed learning can be done when you want it, how you want it.

We hear—more and more—that those diplomas aren't as valuable today as they used to be. But that doesn't negate the truth that being successful at design requires a ton of education.[51]

---

50. And your career will likely plateau early.
51. The general belief, today, is that it requires 10,000 hours of practice to become an expert at anything.

Like any, learning in this field should never stop, and you should never be satisfied that any amount of knowledge is enough.

There's always more to discover: New tools, new digital habits, new consumer expectations. Without an ongoing devotion to learning, the speed of change in the design industry will leave you behind. Just ask anyone who studied paste-up and phototypesetting techniques in design school, right before computers radically changed the industry and turned those fundamentals into relics.

Design school isn't the only path to becoming a designer or staying relevant in the design profession.[52] Regardless of what you study in school (or even whether you went to school or not, like RZA), the most valuable skill you can acquire is the desire to engage with new subjects and apply that knowledge to a wide variety of problems. To approach those problems with a mindset that pulls from many disciplines. The earlier you can do it, the better.

Understanding the concept of "learning to learn" may be the most significant outcome of your design education. It's a tool more valuable than technical proficiency or a strong portfolio. One of my colleagues often says, "you never learn something you don't want to learn."

So becoming a self-learner is all up to you. Prioritize this skill, and you'll have a long (and hopefully successful) career.

---

52. In fact, the U.S. Department of Labor still classifies graphic design as a trade that does not require study at a college or university.

Deadlines are a necessary evil

Learning to ride the waterfall

When you're a student, you tend to work on a single thing for weeks on end. You're enabled to spend only a minimal amount of time on something until it's good enough; good enough for a passing grade, or so that you can focus on other coursework (or, really, any other reason). Or, when given an abundance of time, you focus on pushing pixels until they're perfect.

But, nothing in existence is "perfect." No amount of tweaking ever leads to a fulfilling definition of "done." When you genuinely care about a project, you often become consumed by it. And as soon as satisfaction is attainable, you realize you forgot to write a paper that's due for another class—or you missed a client deadline—and that time spent "perfecting" was just a waste.

That's all well and good when only passing grades are at stake. Unfortunately, if this scenario sounds familiar, you're probably not great at managing your time.

After graduation, many designers start in production-type roles, while high-level concept generation and creative direction fall to more senior staff. Instead of focusing on idea generation, entry-level designers may spend a lot of time on routine tasks, organizing files, and, primarily, executing someone else's concepts.

It takes a varied amount of time for different individuals to prove they're ready to move out of production roles. The ability to execute efficiently, as well as *quickly*, can help accelerate that progression.

Here's an honest fact that I'll keep coming back to: Most design education grads aren't ready for real-world design jobs. Mainly, they aren't prepared for the level of output or quality, or, most importantly, the pace expected of them in a professional setting like an agency.[53]

The reality about pace

Having weeks to work on a project in the "real world" is a rare occurrence. Most designers don't figure this out until the frantic first week at their new job when asked to crank out handfuls of concepts in a day, two, or even hours.

If you're unprepared for that velocity—if you're the type of person that takes forever to pull the first idea out of your head—then you're probably left wondering: Where do I start?

The creative industry is fast-paced, and work flows in a linear direction. In software development, we call this the Waterfall Method: A model that cascades a steady stream of work from initiation to deadline, and allows for minimal schedule flexibility.

---

53. Which I tend to describe as 10x faster than what you're used to in design school.

In addition to this constant race to the finish line, most designers manage multiple clients or projects simultaneously—often with independent deadlines. And, surprise: A couple of those clients will undoubtedly ask you to get something to them early.[54] It's a far cry from design school, where you're focused on one project at a time and not worried about the next until the prior is complete.

Even when you have several weeks to work on something, the amount of time you actually spend "designing it" can only be a fraction of your available time to hit your deadline. Aside from a multitude of things competing for your attention, you've got meetings with teammates and project managers, status updates with your client, and so on for each of your projects or accounts. So you need to develop a solid understanding of how long it will take you to do something—and constantly be aware of what else is on your plate—to balance everything.

I once worked in the publishing industry, where the pace to meet deadlines can be even more intense. I found myself often working on multiple issues of a publication at a time: Concepting layout ideas for a future issue, working through final edits on the prior one, and press checking the one that was about to ship out. And, at the same time, managing other projects for other clients.

Only when I came to the consulting world was I able to narrow my focus to one client at a time. But even now, I'm often not in control of deadlines. I just have to meet them.

It may feel like a blessing that you don't have to worry about these things in design school. As a former student and professor of design, I know how easy it is to get an extension from a professor or permission to turn something in late for a reduced grade.

---

54. Hopefully you work with an account manager that's able to set realistic expectations with clients.

All this does is help you build bad habits. If you miss a deadline in the real world, you could risk losing that client or losing your job.

There are many methods and tools for keeping track of your workload, and you should certainly try out a few until you find the one that works for you.[55] If you don't, you'll just find yourself stressed out and working 60+ hours a week.

Learning to manage

Deadline- and project-management skills will never be picked up in the classroom unless educators move away from assigning sprawling, weeks-long projects.

I prefer to focus on quick exercises and mini-projects that have tight turnarounds in my classroom. I tend to act as a creative director to my young designers. After every project kicks off, I expect to see thumbnail sketches in a day or two. I provide in-progress feedback in the middle of the week, with the final project due not far behind.

If you miss a deadline in my classroom, that's it—no makeup work.

To be honest, some of my students hate this. But I'd rather prepare them for the real world of design than a fantasy world where they can complete work whenever they like. Through this process, they learn how to react to—and act on—feedback, and they discover how to prioritize tasks and refine concepts quickly.

They learn how to manage deadlines.

The only thing missing from this model is the ability to move students through a rotation of design roles—copywriter, art director,

---

55. I prefer using a physical Kanban board with post-it notes to help keep track of the work I need to do, the work I'm doing, and the work I've completed.

production designer—to get the experience of working in a collaborative team environment.[56]

No one loves deadlines, but they're here to stay

It might sound obvious, but sometimes the best way to stay on top of deadlines is just to get started. That's especially true when facing a large workload. I'm not here to help you develop habits; that's something that comes with time and practice.[57]

Personally, I'm always working on things in my head, because creative inspiration can strike at any time. Especially at 6 pm when you're driving home from work or 11 pm when you're trying to get to sleep. Therefore, I'm always working—at least in my mind. And, often, 70% of my work on a given problem takes place in my head before I ever put pencil to paper, or mouse to screen.

That process helps me—you guessed it!—stay on top of deadlines. But it's more heavily related to my personal approach and how I navigate the ideation phase of a project, than an actual "habit." Like Abe Lincoln said, "Give me six hours to chop down a tree, and I will spend four hours sharpening the ax."

As you grow, you'll learn to develop concepts more quickly, and that earlier career question of "Where do I begin?" starts to shift into "Which concept(s) do I move forward with?"

---

56. As a student, one of the smartest things you can do is pursue internships to help you get a first-hand look at how these roles work together in a high-tempo environment.
57. Check out James Clear's book *Atomic Habits* if you need to get better at managing your to-do list.

Sometimes, though, no matter how well you manage your workload, you just can't get ahead. You may get slammed with a new client or need to add a few rush requests on top of your regular workload, and all of a sudden, you're working overtime again.

Quick turnaround is just a hard reality of the job.

So you need to learn to adapt. To expect the unexpected. To be able to jump back-and-forth between clients and tasks. Most importantly, you need to listen to your body and take breaks. Because you're not gonna be at the top of your game unless you come up for air now and then.

No one loves deadlines, but if they didn't exist, we'd have no reason to stop working on anything. Many artists would say they never actually finish a piece; they just eventually have to stop working on it.[58] I guess *that's one way that you are like an artist.*

---

58. Amy Sherald, who painted the official portrait of First Lady Michelle Obama, once said, "every single show I've had for the past three years, the paintings have left my studio wet."

Love what you do, but don't fall in love with it

Falling in love with ideas often leads to heartbreak

While we're growing as designers, we want people to appreciate our work as much as we do. We love all of our ideas, and we give our heart and soul to them. So we, of course, want everyone else to share that same affection.

While seeking this type of surface-level feedback from your friends— or even your peers—may feel good, it's essentially meaningless. Because it often lacks the context appropriate for interpretation; those critical details that separate good from suitable, or successful.

In school, you spend a lot of time perfecting very few ideas; ideas that are hard for you to let go of. Instead of searching for objective feedback, you get stuck by Confirmation Bias: Seeking information that confirms what you already believe about your design rather than feedback that provides a fair, critical analysis of your work.

Because of this, young designers are often defensive when they receive less-than-favorable feedback on something they worked hard on, especially when they feel it's their best work. And it's easy to feel rejected when your designs don't get "picked" during the first few years of your career, which usually means finding yourself working on someone else's idea instead.

But ideas get rejected all the time. No matter how much you love your work, there's a chance most of your ideas will never see the light of day.

And that's ok.

It's ok to have an idea—or a design—rejected, and there's no reason to spend time worrying about it. You can't risk falling in love with the work you produce. On some level, it all needs to be disposable.

The real purpose of design

You see, real-world design has to solve a problem. When we create something, we aren't doing it for ourselves. We have to keep other people (our audience, users, etc.) at the center of our decisions. That's who we're designing for, after all.

The creative process involves generating lots of ideas and then focusing on the ones that best solve our stated problem, not the ones we like the most. That's why I always encourage people to work through ideas on paper, because ideas on paper are easier to throw away.[59]

---

59. We'll talk about how to do this in part 2: Always start with a sketch.

To be honest with your design process, you've got to solicit and accept feedback from others without letting anyone's personal feelings (or agendas) get in the way. Sometimes things just don't work, and you need to know when to pivot.

Today I primarily work in the agile product design space. Agile methodology[60] tells us that we *must be* comfortable throwing things in the trash when feedback proves a design isn't working. And we very often find out that some of the decisions made are wrong. That's cool, because learning you're on the wrong path is a crucial step in getting back on the right one.

When I worked in the agency world—because so much was riding on making a solid first impression with the client—I always felt like there was a lot of pressure to get things right the first time. Designs that clients didn't immediately connect with, or weren't entirely polished, left them saying: What else do you got?[61]

Now that I've learned to rely on feedback from the people actually using the things I (or my teams) design to validate decisions, I feel excellent about getting something 75% right on the first try. That's a big win in my world.

Not staying focused on goals or other methods of measuring the success of your designs (like collecting objective feedback) can lead to lost time, and time is money for everyone involved.[62]

No matter the reason, there's no use spending time trying to salvage an idea that's no longer useful. When you remove your personal feel-

---

60. Software development practices that allow us to stay nimble and focus on constant improvement.
61. This can also be a result of not knowing how to communicate about your work, which we'll cover soon enough.
62. And like money, time can be invested wisely, or wasted foolishly.

ings from the equation, you're more likely to understand (or see) why an idea doesn't work and how to fix it.

Designers who are open to feedback will 100% always end up with a better product; a more successful design.

Why we fall in love with ideas

Ideas generation doesn't come easy for everyone.

When we come across something that could work, we tend to latch onto that idea and hold on for dear life. We let our heart, instead of our head, drive our decisions. And it's really easy to get overly attached to an idea that you put your heart into.

Plus, the creative process can sometimes be slow, and the thought of starting over is scary.

Overconfidence can also drive us to hold onto an idea for too long. If you get too comfortable following your process or let your ego get between you and feedback, you likely won't put in the work to generate alternative ideas or notice when something just isn't working.

If you already fell in love with yourself, or your skills, long before you fell in love with your idea... well, then you've got bigger things to work on.[63] It's just not safe to get attached to these things.

Even though your first idea may ultimately be your best in the long run, seeking feedback will probably make it better, whether it's your first idea or your 100th.

---

63. People don't want to work with jerks who aren't open to objective criticism about their work.

A friend of mine, Mike Mahle, runs his own commercial illustration business. Over the years, he's done work for films produced by Lucasfilm, Warner Brothers, and Disney-Pixar; organizations that are highly protective of the visual representation of their properties. A crucial part of his process when working with them is getting feedback every step of the way.

That means reviewing low- and high-fidelity thumbnail sketches to finalize a concept, all the way to an actor getting approval of how their likeness is depicted in final form. Along the way, any small thing can redirect, stall, or even kill hours of work put into a piece.

He once told me, "It's dangerous to fall in love with your own creations because they will become precious to you." Mourning the death of precious ideas can take its toll.

Learn to let go

Instead, fall in love with the problem you're solving, and the pursuit of ideas that solve it. Fall in love with the idea that you have one of the best jobs on the planet: You get to design things that make people's lives easier, enhance their lifestyle, and on occasion, bring them joy.

Just don't fall in love with the solutions you come up with to solve those problems.

When you're less attached to these things, you'll start to view your work more objectively, analyze it, and be able to create something better in the end.

Learning to let go of *your* favorite work in favor of something that meets user needs or solves the problem on a higher level may be the most challenging lesson a young designer needs to learn.

Design is a business skill

And businesses are eager to leverage design

If you want to be successful in this field, you're gonna need to be able to understand your clients' industries, their competition, and their business goals. Then figure out how to communicate about all of those things.[64]

Once you've done that, you've got to stay focused on those goals and learn to analyze data to measure your effectiveness against them. If you can't already tell, you've chosen a career that's going to throw a lot of new things your way as you progress through it.

But the art school environment of most design programs doesn't stress how important it is to add essential business skills to your toolset. And you probably don't have the extra time, or money, to add

---

64. Collaboration, teaming, and conflict management are important skills to have in a business environment as well.

business courses to your course load. Unfortunately, you're not likely to build any of these skills until after you've graduated.

These are things most designers tend to pick up on the job.

We know that self-expression lies at the core of most art. Very rarely do artists have to pitch their work, ideas, or themselves.[65] Hell, artists can be as eccentric, reticent, or introverted as they please. Sometimes those things even add a welcomed level of mystique to their work.

An artist can pretty much be whoever they want. Period. They create art for their own purposes and don't have to align to any business goals. These are other essential boundaries between artist and designer.[66]

We don't have those luxuries, because art for art's sake doesn't pay the bills in the design world. Instead, we have to be practically skilled and focused on solving problems.

While it's crucial for designers early in their career to hone various design skills, being able to push past the boundaries of the creative world—and really lean into the business world—will make you significantly more effective at your job.[67] Like most, I had to learn these skills the hard way myself.

One of my first design gigs was with a small, non-profit tourism agency, where I was the only creative person in an office of 'business' people. In that role—while early in my career—it took a colossal mindset recalibration to stop thinking about design outcomes as improving the quality of my visual communication skills and start thinking of them in terms of increased tourism dollars.

---

65. Unless we're talking about the commercial art industry.
66. I'm sounding like a broken record by now, but you read the title of the book, right?
67. And more employable.

Learning the ins and outs of the business world was a slow process, and even today, I'm still learning while building relationships with VPs and CTOs of Fortune 500 businesses. Luckily, I have a lot of great people to learn from at my side.

Understanding the business world is essential because your work will almost always have dependencies, and someone is paying you to design something that satisfies them. In most cases, we refer to this as Business Need: The requirements that validate why anyone is spending time on an effort to begin with.

To build confidence, you've got to be able to sell clients on your ability to solve those problems. And a significant way to do that is to show them that you understand both them and their audience, which leads to trust and value in the work you're doing (on both sides).

Good design is good business

A designer's role has evolved tremendously from the era of Paul Rand and Saul Bass, and other 1950s and 60s design pioneers who navigated and shaped the modern age. There's been a progressive shift in perspective from that era's post-World War II optimism that championed the creative genius. Design is no longer seen as an artistic or production-driven discipline focused on big ideas, but rather a culture that breeds business innovation.

The great advantage we have now is that most successful businesses are using design to guide transformation, along with proof of a direct correlation between design-focused organizations and financial growth.[68] It also helps that many of the most successful and well-

---

68. As proven by the McKinsey Design Index, which shows that design-focused organizations increased revenue and shareholder returns at nearly twice the rate of competitors.

known products and services are designed well and provide an excellent user and customer experience.

This concept dates back to the 1970s when Thomas Watson Jr. built the first corporate design program at IBM on the principle that "good design is good business." A concept that Apple borrowed and, in turn, led to its early and sustained success by focusing on personal user experiences that are well- and consistently designed.

Because of these highly-visible outcomes, businesses are eager to lean on design to achieve similar successes, and designers more often have a seat at the table when important business decisions are made. We have access to top-level executives who want to leverage design thinking and human-centered design to balance those decisions. We've even seen the Chief Design Officer role rise at many organizations, from consumer product companies to the financial and automotive industries.

Luckily, we just don't have to work as hard as we used to to sell the value of design.

Instead, we're now faced with learning to speak the language of business, rather than "design speak," so that we can communicate in ways that are familiar to our clients or internal business partners.[69] Genuinely understanding a company, its goals, and how to effectively communicate said goals helps us balance business value and user value, for example, of any solution.[70]

Additionally, designers must develop relationships with stakeholders across client organizations to understand how they work,

---

69. Not the other way around.
70. Or even translate one into the other.

who makes the decisions, and who the true design champions are. The latter being the people we want in our corner from the get-go.

The truth about networking

Yes, we need to talk about networking: A concept that intimidates most introverted designers. I used to be one of them. But networking is very much a business skill. One that sometimes relies on really getting out of your comfort zone.

When I visit university students, I often give a talk that traces my career trajectory. It starts with my senior year in college—when I landed my first design industry internship—and leads up to where I'm at today.

A throughline of that journey is that every opportunity I've had— whether full-time or freelance—happened because of a connection I made or a client I impressed along the way.

The unfortunate truth of many jobs is that you need to know someone to get hired. Don't mistake that truth for nepotism, or favoritism. It's just absolutely crucial that you get out in the real world and make connections. You don't need to have a family member or a friend-of-a-friend in high places to get hired for your dream job. Get that idea out of your head.

You simply need to be open to meeting new people, having conversations, collaborating, and seeing what you can learn from one another.

That doesn't have to be done 100% in person. LinkedIn is a great starting point, that many before you didn't have, to connect with others in your field—or even hiring managers at your dream company— and start developing relationships.

A single connection can take you miles beyond your physical location.

We tend to think of networking as a bunch of strangers in a room forced to communicate with one another over drinks.[71] That's not always the case, and at least, it certainly doesn't have to be.

Networking is a practice you should start early on in your journey with your peers at school. Later, attend events hosted by local agencies or sponsored by design organizations. Join Slack communities. Travel to conferences or seek out meetup groups (in person or online). Listen to what these people have to say when you do this, and learn from them.

And when you do, you're already building your first business skills.

---

71. I don't have any interest in that, either.

Don't sweat the critique

Good design is measurable

Almost every project you'll work on in school allows for creative freedom—and time—to experiment. Unfortunately, little happens to measure the success of most projects outside of meeting deadlines, staying within the expectations of the assignment instructions, and reacting to any feedback received during critiques.

Ugh, design school critiques. We really need to talk about how problematic they are.

In my opinion, they're often a wasted exercise. Typical critiques are rarely conducted in a format that allows for an objective discussion of the work, and students aren't coached in more valuable ways to participate in them. Fundamental issues like audience and meaning often take a backseat to aesthetics.

This misdirected purpose often leads to a wholly different critique of design assignments from the one students encounter when critiquing design history. It's no wonder, then, that many young designers are not only incapable of presenting a convincing argument for their work but are equally incapable of processing useful feedback from clients and peers.

As a teacher and student I've seen many models, and very few good ones in practice. My least favorite is the notorious "3x format" where you travel around the room as each student, in turn, shares a comment first on something they like, second on something they don't like, and then finishes with a piece of advice. This format leaves the presenting student with an overabundance of feedback to consider, much of which they'll probably just shut out.

So students fall back on routine responses such as "what bothers me is..." or "I like that..." without any deeper reflection on the real success of a solution beyond personal preference. When critiques lack proper guidance on what observers should focus attention on, it's no wonder that these ceremonies lead to mostly aesthetic-based discussion.

To help combat wasted critiques, I have my students begin by stating their goals for a project and then outlining the process for accomplishing those goals—what they researched, how they weighed decisions—and whether or not they feel their solution is successful.

Suppose someone in the group has objective criticism. In that case, they're only allowed to share it in the form of a problem statement. That small directive turns common responses like "I think you should make the type smaller" into something more valuable like "I feel the type size draws attention away from the important information."

This exercise aims to rule out subjectivity and help them navigate feedback from real clients, who often come to the table with solutions—rather than focusing on a problem and allowing the designer to distill that feedback into actionable items. It also helps them remove the phrase "I like" from their vocabulary.

Where's the proof?

While this makes for shorter, more objective critique exercises, it doesn't provide students with any tools to measure a project's real success outside of the grade they earn or the confirmation they receive.[72]

All designers should want their work to have an impact. As problem solvers and process improvers by nature, we're less accepting of bad design when we encounter it in our daily lives. We recognize the power good design has to improve so many things.

But beyond that surface-level appreciation—all the warm fuzzies, the awards publications, and the social media likes—we still have to be able to connect the value of a design to its goals.[73] It's up to us to make sure that we turn every project, and every decision, into a success story that's backed up by data, whether that's through qualitative or quantitative feedback.

Through these efforts of measure, we're able to prove the valuable role that design contributes to business success. And the more work we do to build a proven track record for the business value of design, the more we'll be able to elevate our craft.

Measuring with numbers

So how do you know if a design is successful? It starts with clear goals.

To set yourself up for measurable success, you first need to lay down the metrics you're trying to improve—or your primary goal of accomplishment—so that actual data can back up the end solution.

---

72. Or outside of additional feedback they receive from me.
73. Sure, everyone likes the attention that comes with awards competitions and design annuals, but that's often a mere celebration of novelty.

This is why creative briefs—documents that clearly outline the problem that needs to be solved—exist. They provide a synopsis of core business objectives, deadlines, audience, etc., along with any necessary context and background we should be aware of. Think of it as a blueprint that helps guide strategy and keeps everyone aligned to the same goals.

Creative briefs help set clear objectives and outline expectations upfront. When *all* of these things are made clear, it's easier to determine what was or wasn't accomplished when a project is complete.

But that's obviously not the only way to know, and even creative briefs can be subjective.[74]

Web designers often set up KPIs[75] to track data like the number of products sold or the number of new member signups, and keep an eye on negative metrics like the number of users abandoning the sign-up process. Web banners are validated through quantifiable data like click-through and retention rates. You get the idea.

But while this type of data tells you *what's* happening, it doesn't tell you why. When testing the success of a product feature, for example, data can tell you what someone did but not *why* they did it.

Measuring with feelings

Design thinking and agile methodology are, in theory, cyclical processes. They treat every feature—every interaction—of a product, process, or experience as something with potential for improvement. No matter how often you measure the work, it's never truly finished.

---

74. For example, if the primary business goal of a creative brief is to increase ROI, then you better make it rain, or else your client may not see the same win that you do.
75. Key Performance Indicators.

Management leader Peter Drucker said, "if you can't measure it, you can't improve it." To many, this means it's impossible to know if a design is successful if you didn't first define what success looks like. Otherwise, the safest business decision is to focus time and resources on something else that *can* be measured.

UX designers rely on qualitative methods like usability studies and surveys to measure the human success factor; the data that tells us when something is easy to use and how satisfying it actually is.[76] By running controlled scenarios that focus on the user and their goals, UX designers can understand if a feature helps users achieve their goals *and* how they feel during and after the activity.

When assessing an existing product, designers often want to start by identifying problems. They'll conduct a heuristic evaluation to identify usability issues and prioritize addressing them based on evidence, rather than opinion.[77]

Once those issues are managed, it's time for a usability study!

In 2010 Google launched their HEART framework for measuring user experience on a large scale. It relies on the following qualitative and quantitative categories: **Happiness** (how people feel about a product), **Engagement** (how people are using it), **Adoption** (creation of new user accounts), **Retention** (sustained use of the product), and **Task Success** (users successfully completing actions).

These metrics can be applied from the top-level product down to a single feature, and they give Google teams a common framework for objective measurement based on statistical, behavioral, and attitudinal data.

---

76. Sometimes quantitative methods are involved too.
77. A common model to follow is Jakob Nielsen's "10 Usability Heuristics for User Interface Design."

No matter what methods or tools you use to measure design success, can any of them tell us about the *quality* of our design?

Every designer will develop their own understanding of what good design *looks* like. It's not easily qualifiable. Internally-led evaluations will always be problematic because personal bias can creep in, and surveys can lead to blind spots or disconnect between a user and an experience.

By incorporating critique and data collection as an essential part of your practice, you'll be able to grow faster and make design decisions quicker.[78] And be able to replace your concerns about "good" with an understanding of "successful."

So don't be afraid of data. More data means more insight, leading to more informed design decisions.[79] Regardless of what you're working on, choose a measurement method that will help you do better work, keep you in check, and help you show—in the end—how design can lead the way to make an impact.

And when you're done, socialize that data with other people to help tell your success story.

---

78. Establishing clear goals will have the same effect.
79. And helps you avoid opinion-based decisions.

Ideas don't sell themselves

You do

When I was a student, I assumed a career in design meant sitting in front of a computer all day pushing pixels around until they were perfect. After a solid 8-10 hours of that, I'd throw my leather messenger bag over my shoulder and grab a coffee to reflect on all the cool stuff I made that day.

I never imagined I would ultimately spend so little time designing and so much time *talking* about design. So I quickly realized that the ability to speak about my work confidently would have a massive impact on my career growth, allowing me to build more strategic relationships and pursue the opportunities I desired rather than constantly staying on the hustle.

When it comes to selling ideas, I'm not talking about the power of persuasion or the art of working a room. Nothing as superficial as flashy showmanship. I'm talking about confidence in yourself and your abilities as a designer and storyteller.

Sooner or later in your career, you'll have to show your body of work—or your ideas for a particular project—to a client or a recruiter and convince them that you know what you're doing. To sell not only the solution and your expertise, but the value that both bring.

To do this, you need to not only understand your clients' goals, but you need to be able to articulate them—along with how you plan to achieve those goals with a creative solution—in a way they understand. The success of any potential work you do depends on your ability to align partners to a shared vision. And, often, your vision is one of many others they need to weigh, as potential clients will be evaluating how your "pitch" stacks up against those of other potential designers.

So, with no data yet available as measurable proof, how do you go about persuading someone that your ideas are any good?

The work does not speak for itself

You've probably heard the phrase "good design speaks for itself." What a dumb thing to say.

In theory, presenting work sounds simple enough, but the most brilliant design solution can quickly become a wasted idea if it isn't clearly and articulately communicated. Remember, we're dealing with real humans here, so we need to appeal to their senses when advocating for our ideas.

In the design world, the most successful communicators don't consider themselves salespersons: They're storytellers. So as you transition from student to professional, it's important to stop talking about your work in terms of aesthetic or technical choices and learn to tell stories about solutions and outcomes.

Because your clients likely don't give a shit about fonts or the nuances of color theory. They aren't going to be impressed by your understanding of design history or the fact that you have a lot of social media followers. They want to hear those success stories we covered in the last conversation: How you solved problems similar to theirs for other clients and how you measured those successes.[80]

Getting someone to understand your idea is only table stakes; it's the bare minimum you need to accomplish. People naturally want to be entertained and inspired. So, more importantly, you need to get them aligned with your idea *and* get excited about it.

That's where good storytellers excel.

Here's my advice: Start by familiarizing yourself with your audience. Get to know their interests and backgrounds to understand how to connect with them. Remember those goals we talked about developing? Now is the time to re-articulate them and communicate your plan to stay focused on and accomplish them. By understanding your audience's desires and motivations, you'll be more likely to communicate in a way they understand[81] and potentially connect to something that will help them say, "I get it!"[82]

Showing clients you genuinely understand and care about what motivates them builds trust. And trust goes a long way in this industry. Afterward, kick that project's ass and you should have another success story at your disposal to share with the next client, and the next.

---

80. If you only have a portfolio of student work at your disposal, don't worry! We'll talk about how to turn those into success stories in the next conversation.
81. And once you crack that message: Practice, practice, practice.
82. And don't forget that they have valuable opinions as well. Be open to hearing them out when they have suggestions and questions.

Bring artifacts to the table

Beyond solid communication skills, you need to learn how to craft a concrete presentation. And, yes, this probably means that you'll need to work in PowerPoint from time to time. In many scenarios, you'll be sending that document to the client as a follow-up, so working in programs that are familiar to them is just another example of speaking their language.

But you don't need to spend hours slaving over a presentation deck.

Regardless of the tool, any idea can—and should—be communicated through simple visuals. As long as you take the time to polish your thoughts and focus on finding the story to express them. The purpose of creating a presentation deck isn't to focus on perfect design artifacts. The story (and the deck) should stay focused on the value the idea—or ideas—will deliver to the client and their business.

Bringing the story and visuals together should only help you advocate for things in the best way possible, capturing and holding their attention and interest.

One of my favorite design world stories is how George Lois—art director for Esquire in the 60s and 70s and creator of the "I Want My MTV" campaign of the 1980s—apparently got Goodman's Matzos to approve a campaign they didn't like. After rejecting his idea, he leaned out the window of their New York office building and threatened to jump if they didn't trust him, saying, "You make the matzos, I'll make the ads!"

It certainly makes for a compelling story.

But the days of the reckless creative genius are over.[83] It's implausible that clients are going to take a gamble just because you said, "trust me." Very few names carry enough weight in this business to inspire people to just hand over budget dollars for campaigns they're unsure about.

Today, we need to rely on clear communication to get client support rather than resort to more dramatic tactics.

How do I find clients, anyway?

We should probably take a step back and think about an important question: How do I attract clients in the first place? That is a common topic of interest from students looking to build their portfolios or explore the world of freelancing.

Whether you end up running your own design business or working as another cog in the machine of a large organization, you're still a representative for the design practice of that org. So don't assume that you have to be the one calling all the shots to build the type of meaningful relationships that turn into partnerships.

Honestly, you never know where work is going to come from. If you're good at building relationships and delivering above expectations, then a lot of it will probably come through referrals. And you should always feel fortunate when that happens, even though it's a direct result of your hard work.

But relying on referrals isn't a good long-term strategy to follow because it's unpredictable and inconsistent. A better approach is intentionally marketing yourself as an expert in the industry you want

---

83. Sadly, I might add. Those seemed like fun times.

to focus on and crafting a suitable personal story to communicate that expertise.

As individual contributors, I believe we should all strive to be versatilists: People who can wear many hats, as they say. But when it comes to organizations—whether it be a global design agency or a small freelance business—the ones specializing are bound to win more often than not.

So if there's a particular client you're looking to land or a specific industry you want to build a practice in, you need to develop and promote yourself as an expert in that industry to make it happen.

If you want to, say, build a practice that only works with healthcare organizations, then you'll not only need to lean heavily on experts in that field, but you'll want to do a lot of networking and take the time to immerse yourself in that culture.[84] Learn as much as you can about the modern healthcare system and the players in its ecosystem.[85]

Whatever your desired niche is, once you identify it you can always start to carve out more categories and build a solid portfolio that backs up your expertise in a given industry and its offshoots.

Case in point: For several years, I worked at an agency called Market-Place: The Food Marketing Agency, a studio founded by a husband and wife with many years of business-to-business (B2B) food and beverage industry experience. When they went into business together, that's where they decided to focus; leveraging the relationships they already had in that world.

Successful work in B2B led to expansion into the business-to-consumer (B2C) space developing brands and packaging for the

---

84. And work on building a client base in that industry.
85. And probably hire some of those people to work for you.

consumer market. And that, in turn, led to expansion into the pet care and, eventually, health and wellness industries. All of this took time—and was accomplished step-by-step—but it all started with a specific focus.

Today, to signify that growing expertise, they are known as Market-Place: The Food, Pet, and Wellness Marketing Agency.

The point of sharing this is: Potential clients won't evaluate you on a beautiful portfolio alone. You communicate the actual value of your work by building relationships, delivering exceptionally, and celebrating successes.

A relationship built on trust and rapport is where it begins. You inspire people to want to work with you by communicating your expertise, the way you think, and the ways you solve problems for other clients.

That's how you sell the value of design today. Not by threatening to jump out of windows like George Lois.

Your portfolio doesn't define you

People hire people, not portfolios

By now, you're probably thinking, "I need to focus on a *hell of a lot* of stuff to be successful in this industry." Things like staying aligned to goals, focusing on outcomes, defining and measuring success. Your portfolio is the one place where all those skills come together to tell your personal story: Who you are as a designer.

But it can't do that work by itself.

Whether you're on the hunt for an internship, your first full-time job after college, or looking to make a mid- to late-career move, your portfolio is only a foot in the door. And the people in charge of hiring should only view it through the lens of "is this person capable of doing the work we expect of them?"

Most of the time, that answer is "probably."

That's the point of the interview process: To truly understand competency.[86] So you need to look at the process of developing your portfolio as a strategic way to get those interviews.

No matter the situation, you're trying to get hired to work in a field that's guaranteed to change, and it's a mistake to believe that your portfolio can tell everything about your capabilities as a designer. How you empathize with people, the way you think about design, your ability to lead a discussion and communicate about the work you do: These are things that can only be validated by having a conversation with someone.

I didn't gain much insight into this reality until I started the interview process with more strategic and people-focused organizations. Before that, the recruiters and creative directors I interviewed with only evaluated *me* by looking at my work. They were more interested in how they could benefit from what I'd already accomplished, so I rarely had opportunities to discuss my career through anything other than a rearview mirror.

The better I got at crafting my personal success stories and putting them into a visual format, I found myself spending less time discussing my portfolio during interviews. Not because my portfolio was perfect, but because I understood who I was and what type of work I wanted to do in the future. My portfolio reflected what I'd accomplished, but I could just as competently communicate what I'd learned from that work through conversation.

Design is an intelligent enterprise, so designers should be skeptical of interviewers who are more focused on evaluating their aesthetic capabilities than understanding how their brain works. Through

---

86. And, in many cases, to determine culture fit.

many years of varied interview tactics, that revelation led to a complete re-evaluation of how I approach portfolio creation with students *and* interview candidates today.

Most portfolios are problematic

Throughout the years, I've reviewed lots of portfolios compiled from the work of both students and design veterans. Reviewing the former can often be a frustrating process (to say the least).[87]

Once you see enough student portfolios, you know exactly what to expect: A lot of typography exercises, ads for hypothetical products, branding campaigns for made-up businesses, redesigns for already successful interfaces, fake app prototypes, and concert posters (always concert posters). And when you go through student portfolios, it's often easy to separate the class projects from the real ones.

In reality, there are only two things I need to evaluate your design skill through your portfolio alone effectively. One is the quality of execution, and the other is a straightforward decision-making process for each project. These two things work best in tandem.

The fundamental issue with most portfolios is that they only focus on the former—making the work look good in presentation—and do not provide insight into the problem or the decision-making process that led to the solution. Pretty images alone make it impossible to evaluate a designer's skill fairly, and make it a lot easier to disqualify someone as a candidate.

But it goes beyond my own understanding. You need to give the impression that *you* clearly understand how to frame a problem. Can

---

87. The worst, of which, are the speed-dating-style design reviews that take place at student conferences.

you turn your process into a compelling narrative? How do you make decisions? Are you capable of reflecting on outcomes?

Good work needs context.

So here are a few facts I want to clarify: It doesn't matter how well you present your work unless the "how" and "why" of that final design are made clear. I haven't seen a physical portfolio in years, so don't waste your time putting together a traditional "book" unless you have work that truly shines in three dimensions. Otherwise, a digital portfolio is much more manageable, shareable, and scalable. And it doesn't matter if you present it through a website, a PDF, a Figma prototype, or a Behance link.

The delivery format is up to you, and most won't care which you choose. When I help students put portfolios together—or when I review potential candidates—I expect only three things: Show process, give context, and keep it simple.

Process

I want to see the path from idea to execution when it comes to process. Whether that's mood boards full of inspiration, thumbnail sketches, storyboards... it doesn't matter as long as you're showing me that you followed a process that put "pencil to paper" rather than jumping straight to the magic computer screen.

These are the details that make me smile when I see them incorporated into someone's portfolio. They show me how that person nurtures and evolves an idea or pivots and reacts to feedback when a different path arises.

Unfortunately, most students overlook how important it is to record the early phases of a project and often throw away artifacts that give insight into thoughts and workflow. It doesn't matter how low-fidelity these items are as long as they provide insight into the design process. So throw in prototypes and wireframes, scrapped directions, thumbnail sketches, anything that adds to the holistic picture.

Sure, a good process doesn't always lead to good design, but it usually leads to good design thinking. Strategic thinkers will always have the upper hand in this world.

Context

Images of your work don't communicate the necessary context on their own. If I'm just looking at something, I'm probably going to have more questions than anything else. So include short descriptive sentences that give insight into the problem statement and the solution path. Focus on the most interesting and impactful parts of the project.

If a piece in your portfolio didn't lead to any tangible result, why include it to begin with? You'd have no story to tell. Presenting the story behind each project is the best way to communicate the problems and outcomes of your process. People want to see case studies, so figure out how to put one together.

Big images look great, but they can't inherently tell what problem was solved, or how. Instead, frame those images within a case study that outlines your process. Articulate what you tried, what worked, and what didn't.[88] A thoughtful case study should provide insight into the "how" and "why" behind your decisions. That's a fundamental component to evaluating your work on screen, to determine if that next step conversation should occur.

---

88. Also, how long did the project take from start to finish and what was your role? Always be honest if you weren't working alone.

Treat the projects you showcase as an arc in your personal story; a narrative that describes your journey as a designer. Because your portfolio isn't a scrapbook, it's a pitch deck for selling your skills.

Most of your student projects will only prove that you're able to follow a prompt unless you put in the extra effort to frame the problem. So you must avoid saying things like "for this assignment we were instructed to… " and instead move toward crafting the message as "the goals for this project were…"

If positive results exist, you better detail them.

Simplicity

The concept of simplicity is easy in theory but one of the most difficult in practice: You don't need to include everything you've ever done. Some people will tell you to incorporate less than ten projects; some will say they only want to see your three strongest pieces. There's no magic number. Just stick to your strongest work or the work that can tell a great story.

Your portfolio, as a student, should be representative of the best things you've done up to that point. As your career progresses, you may decide to highlight specific skills, a style, or a specialization, and your portfolio will evolve, but you should always prioritize simplicity.

The goal is to emphasize quality over quantity.

And try only to showcase real work. Unsolicited redesigns for big brands may get you followers on Instagram, but if your only goal for redesigning a logo is "I thought it would be fun," then there's no story to be told. Unsolicited redesigns are only valuable if you're tackling a real problem that exists.

Once you write your story, challenge yourself to edit it down. You started with 500 words, but can you tell the same story with 250? Ultimately, don't spend too much time talking about any one project or aspect of a single project. If it takes you 45 minutes to effectively cover a single piece in your portfolio during an interview, that's not a good representation of practical communication skills.

And don't overdesign your portfolio. Let the work be the focus; don't clutter other design elements around it.

The conversation is key

The goal is to give a recruiter or hiring manager (or client) just enough to catch their attention and make them want to talk to you in person. It's a delicate balance.

In the end, be prepared to talk about all of your work. The portfolio can only get your foot in the door, and once there, you need to sell it yourself. So practice and be prepared for questions.

Having that conversation with someone is the best way to show them what it's like to work with you without having worked with you. So all of these portfolio-building tactics need to come together—along with the way you communicate about yourself, where you've been, and where you want to go—to define who you are as a designer.

If your portfolio shows that you're able to work with people, stick to deadlines, and deliver successful work, then you're probably going to get those opportunities.[89]

You'll be able to add flavor during these conversations that tell someone what's unique about you and your background: How you got into

---

89. Or land those clients.

design, what skills you've developed and the ones you plan to work on, what your interests are, and the unique perspective you can bring to their organization, etc.

You don't need a perfect portfolio to get a job. Your personality will help fill in some of those gaps during the interview process.

Creating a valuable portfolio takes a lot of time and effort, but it's worth both. Just remember that people shouldn't want to hire you only for the things you've done, but for what you are likely capable of doing with them in the future.

Don't work for free

Your time and skill have value

You need work to build a portfolio, and you need a solid portfolio to get clients. That's the catch-22 that most young designers will struggle with: You need experience to gain experience.

Throughout your career, especially when starting out, you *will* be asked to work for free. And accepting those opportunities may seem like the answer to that problem; a lucrative chance for you to start building your portfolio with work for actual "clients."

I'll put this one pretty bluntly: If someone asks you to work for free, it means they don't appreciate what you're capable of doing. And if someone doesn't appreciate you, they likely won't appreciate the free work you do for them. So just save yourself the hassle.

People who are well-skilled in *any* profession deserve to be paid and respected. Not only for the value and perspective they bring to their industry, but the hard work they put in to build that expertise. In truth, many clients tend to think they are paying for outcomes and deliverables—ads, websites, experiences—but what they're really paying for is your expertise, your knowledge, and *your* experience.[90]

Working for free undermines the quality of all these things and won't lead to an accurate representation of your design capabilities. Even when your skills are green, they still have value. You shouldn't let anyone take them for granted.

So don't do it unless you have an excellent reason.[91] And in my opinion, an unpaid internship is not a good one, regardless of the knowledge you could gain.

From time to time, some designers will take on pro-bono work for friends or family, or causes they value. Many people volunteer time to charity organizations or serve on not-for-profit boards, and choosing to donate your design time to things that you care about—or make you feel fulfilled—is no different. That's something entirely on you to decide.

Personally, I don't like the idea of money exchanging hands between friends. It just complicates things. So if a buddy has a solid idea that seems worthwhile of your time, go for it. Just make sure they know that you control the timeline and that you're expecting their trust in return. If not, tell them you're too busy. You should never feel obligated to do work you don't want to do.

Money certainly isn't the only form of value or reward for your work. But more often than not, the prospect of working for free doesn't result in any actual value for either party.

---

90. Keep these things in mind if you're trying to determine what to charge someone for freelance work.
91. Check out this handy chart, made by Jessica Hische, to determine if a project is valuable enough to you to do it for free: ShouldIWorkForFree.com.

It's not just about you

Free work devalues the design market. Not just your work, but the work of your peers as well.

Every time a designer chooses to provide free work or significantly lower their rates to win a project, it becomes more difficult for other designers to compete. Why would someone pay any of us if someone else is willing to do the work for nothing?

Design is a business; a profession. And you have to treat it like one. Agreeing to do free work reinforces the idea that design is somehow less inherently valuable than other professions. Plumbers don't work for free. Neither do architects. Why should you?

The more you say no to these opportunities, the more you strengthen the future market for all designers.

Those first few years when you're a young, hungry creative will be your most vulnerable. People know this, so they'll try to get free work out of you by promising the things you feel like you need most at the time: Experience, portfolio pieces, relationships that lead to paid work in the future. You've got to be smart enough to resist these attempts to take advantage of your skills.

The following are a few things, in particular, to avoid.

Spec work

Spec work is the request to present a design idea with no defined compensation—ranging from low-fidelity concepts to fully-developed campaign directions. Partaking in spec work is akin to entering a lottery, with the potential reward of being paid to do work you've already been doing. It's a wholly client-driven concept that allows businesses to test drive a designer's skills while competing against peers.

Spec work often leads to little return on the time, effort, and guess-work that goes into a chance of blindly impressing a potential client. Surprisingly, many businesses still request that even the most prominent agencies pitch ideas for free when responding to RFPs, sometimes requiring in-person presentations that are scored and ranked on narrow criteria.

Sure, if they like the work you did or appreciate the effort you showed, they may decide to compensate you for that work (on their terms) and maybe even hire you. But in most cases, you're just wasting time developing ideas for free that will never see the light of day.[92]

There's often little value in working with these types of clients, to begin with, as they're probably focused on *what they want* versus giving an expert time to truly understand *what they need.* So decisions are made with little insight.

Also, be cautious of anyone who asks you to do a spec project as a test for employment. That happens way more than you'd think.

Early in my career, I got called back for a second interview for a staff design position with a small not-for-profit organization. They handed me an ad spec sheet and pointed me to a computer when I arrived. I'd heard about test projects before—and received advice that I should avoid them—but I really wanted this job, so I rolled with it.

When it was all over, I found out that they had an ad deadline to meet and decided to use my second "interview" to test my skill and get some free work out of me in one sitting. And if I remember correctly,

92. Check out NoSpec.com for a thorough review on the evils of spec work.

that was it: I designed the ad, and I was free to go. They didn't even have additional questions for me.

I shouldn't have let them take advantage of my time and talent, and neither should you. If I were more mature, I probably would have spoken up or even said, "no thank you." I ended up taking that job but never forgot about that experience, and made a note never to do it again.

Exposure

We all experience this one at some point: Clients with no budget who offer "exposure" as compensation. I can only recall a single instance of this from my career. Someone asked me to design a commemorative plaque for a monument. It was for a great cause, I'm sure, but a very low-stakes, low-visibility need. They had no money to pay me, but the opportunity for exposure was too good to pass up from their point of view!

I politely declined.

The thing with exposure is: It doesn't pay the bills. As a young designer, you'll never be able to fill your stomach, or keep the lights turned on, with exposure.[93]

The only way exposure could ever lead to the success promised is if the organization offering it has a massive commercial presence. But then that would mean they probably have plenty of money to pay you, too.

It doesn't take a rocket surgeon to realize that no one offering you exposure is likely to have the following or social media presence to deliver on it.

---

93. You can't do these things with "likes," either.

Design contests

Anyone offering you a prize for a logo, package design, book cover—even if that prize is the publication of said book cover—is just coming at you from another angle to get something for free.

Companies like 99designs and Fiverr turn design into a commodity by seemingly providing a place where anyone can purchase design services through a contest model. And, honestly, clients may come away from these sites with some decent work. It's not so much an issue of quality as it is one of methods and motivations.

Businesses are given ground to put many designers through several rounds of revisions, with only the "winning" designer paid for any of their time and work. That could number in the tens or hundreds of unpaid designers receiving no fair pay per project.

Designers who contribute to these contest models are working against the goals and interests of our profession: Often chasing trends to capture clients' interests, creating work that is derivative to save time, or outright stealing other people's work to make an easy paycheck.

Participating in crowdsourcing contest models only perpetuates unrealistic expectations on the level of effort, skill, and time involved to execute an effective design solution.

True story: I once worked on a branding campaign for a consumer packaged bakery company. After presenting a single round of logo directions, the client returned with their own version and said: "Can we try something like this?" A quick Google search took me to a 99designs contest page with several similar—but slightly different iterations—on the logo the client sent me, which was also present, and identified as the contest winner.

It turns out they first ran a design contest to decide on a logo and then came to the agency I was working for to get our thoughts on it and maybe polish it up. But they waited until we'd already put a considerable amount of research and time into the direction for the brand to mention it.

Talk about wasting time and money: They did it twice!

While you're avoiding all these things—spec work, design contests, and other compensation-free opportunities—you can stay focused on more productive activities to elevate your skills and career. Things like networking, or writing, or building something of your own. Instead of saying yes to free work, say yes to yourself and the activities that keep you focused on your desired career growth.

There's no fame in this game

Design isn't about the designer

We spend a lot of time in design school studying the history of our profession and digging into the portfolios of successful designers from the past. The people that defined and shaped the early design landscape.

So it's natural to respect the big names from design history—people like Paul Rand, Massimo Vignelli, Seymour Chwast—as not only a source of inspiration, but for the perceived level of fame that history has placed upon them. A class that many aspiring designers wish to achieve.

Honestly, who doesn't want a little piece of fame these days? Desiring that type of reward is human nature that's only heightened in the digital age.

When I was a student, I had the chance to meet and talk with Pop artist Ed Paschke. That was like a hero moment for me, finding myself in conversation with an artist that I'd written papers on; that I'd read about in history books.[94] But does that mean anything to *you*?

True fame in most industries is difficult to attain. And if you do, what does it really mean?

Stefan Sagmeister (a "famous" designer by all accounts) has, on numerous occasions, stated, "a famous designer is like a famous electrician." Meaning that true fame is difficult to codify in this profession, as we often influence culture and public opinion behind the scenes.[95]

If you're looking for fame—the real kind, not the social media kind—this probably isn't the right profession for you.

What is fame in this industry?

Design is our own private world, and most people outside of it are wholly unaware of who we are. People like Aaron Draplin and Jessica Hische may be the star personalities of our world today. Still, those outside it are just as unfamiliar with who they are—or what they've done—as most people outside the art world are of Ed Paschke.

In preparation for this book, I came across an article titled "The World's Most Famous Graphic Designers in 2021." I'd never heard of 90% of them, although I'm sure they all do fantastic work. The ones I did know: It was because they tend to publish and share knowledge—to help shape discussion and awareness of our profession—not because of their body of work.

---

94. Ed was one of those artists just famous enough to get a page devoted to himself in a comprehensive overview of 20th century art, but not on the level of household name.
95. Unlike rock stars and actors.

So if this idea—that you probably won't become the next famous designer—is accurate, then why do all of these familiar names keep popping up in history books and class lectures?

Many of the designers you know from history paved the way in articulating what makes design great (and valuable) before others could by directly influencing the early formation of design theory. Like the forefathers of the United States, we remember them as pioneers. It's unlikely that you would know the name Josef Müller-Brockmann today if someone else had beaten him to publishing a seminal work on grid systems, or Jan Tschichold if he hadn't embraced and championed the Swiss style so early.

All of these people had something to say; something new to contribute. They took risks like Alan Fletcher or broke the rules like David Carson. They championed the birth of a movement like Paul Rand or new technology like April Greiman.

Or even shaped an entire industry like Claude Garamond.

What's more important?

Students often get caught up in the idea that they have to develop a style, a signature look, or a process for their work to help them stand out and define who they are as a designer. To this, I often respond with, "name ten famous designers working today and describe their style for me."

I can probably only provide three names and examples myself, and I've been doing this for almost 20 years.

So if you're drawn to design because you want to have half a million followers on Instagram like Jessica Walsh or because you saw Timothy Goodman's Sharpie art on the cover of *Fortune*, then your motivations are a little misguided. Because the world of magazine covers doesn't have room for a lot of Sharpie artists, but there's plenty of room for versatile storytellers and problem solvers that most people have never heard of.

The goal here is to approach any problem, solve it appropriately, and do it with confidence and expertise. It's more about each client's individual needs than it is about any one designer's style.

Possession of a wide variety of skills is what pays the bills consistently.

If you focus your design education on becoming good at one thing— to be known for it—then no one is going to hire you unless they are in desperate need of that one thing. That's a fact.

PART TWO

Becoming the next design iteration of you

While part one focused on the truths of the design profession, part 2 is full of anecdotes, advice, and insight—mostly centered around failures and successes from my career and the lessons I learned. It's full of inspiration to kickstart your personal creative process, build additional skills that make you a more dynamic designer, ideas for improving your working relationships with people, and—hopefully—concepts that will help you form a deeper level of thinking and understanding about the world of design.

In his book *Feck Perfuction,* designer and artist James Victore wrote, "This gift of creativity makes us powerful but also awkward, weird, and vulnerable." This next part of the journey should help connect you—or reconnect you—to that weird, creative side so you can unleash your authentic self in your work life.

True design innovation comes from unexpected places, experiences, and points of view. So let's take a stab at engaging your wonder and curiosity. Exploring these ideas together should challenge you to think deeper; to help you understand what makes you, you.

Now that you know what's expected of you as a designer, let's find out what you're capable of.

Surviving the freelance game

The lessons I learned working for myself

Many of us come out of design school not knowing what we'll do next. That post-graduation period can be tough to navigate and is often heightened by the realization that job offers aren't as plenty as you expected (or you haven't looked too hard yet).

But most of us faced with the reality of entering the job market are aware of two things: We need to build experience, and we need to build a portfolio. So the answer for many is: "I'll just freelance!" Problem solved.

Going into business for yourself might seem like a solid enough plan at the time. "I'll tell people I'm a designer. And they'll probably need some design, so they'll pay me to design stuff." But let's be honest: The average kid coming out of art school doesn't know much about business. And even if they do, it takes time to build a steady flow of clients and work to support themself as a full-time freelancer.

Anyone who successfully made the jump straight from student to freelancer will tell you that it takes way more than just a laptop and some social media accounts. More often than not, it quickly becomes a "what the hell have I gotten myself into?" situation.

That's why I advise designers entering the workforce to give full-time employment *and* freelancing as a side hustle a shot. Try them both out for a while to see which feels right. This allows you to enjoy the comfort of full-time employment (also known as a steady paycheck and health insurance) while building a personal client base; to test the waters before jumping to freelancing full-time.

And—if you can swing both—*you may find that this* model will suit you for longer than you expect. I did it, and here's what I learned.

Every project won't be valuable, but every experience will be

A lot of people like to brag about their atypical career paths. How they went from industry to industry before discovering their passion for design (or whatever). That's not me.

I started working at a local print shop, making plates for large-scale offset presses, running digital printing presses, and doing pre-press desktop work.[1] Hell, I even spent time on the warehouse floor running binding machines and sweeping up when work was slow. After a three-year-stint at a not-for-profit design gig, I was able to break into the

---

1. Pre-press work is essentially taking someone's design files and setting them up to be print-ready.

agency world, where I spent ten years working in publishing, branding, consumer package design, and user experience.

I eventually ended up at a global consulting firm where I led product development for Fortune 500 companies, and now I run a product design team in the health tech industry. Where I'm at today is a long way from that print shop—and days spent inhaling second-hand chemical fumes—but design has always been at the center of my world from start to finish.

Along the way, I always freelanced. Until recent years, when I finally hit a point in my work/life balance that supporting freelance clients—in a way that was valuable to both parties—was no longer possible or desirable.

And when I reflect on how and where my freelance journey began, it's difficult to say who benefitted the most from my early relationships and experiences.

When I was at that print shop—and tangentially finishing up my undergrad education—there was a global vacuum cleaner brand headquartered right down the street from me.[2] One day—I shit you not—I pulled a tab off of a bulletin board flier; a "help wanted" ad looking for freelance designers. I hadn't considered it too strongly at this point but figured, "why not?" So I gave the number a call and spent the next few months doing package illustrations for that company's various vacuum cleaner and accessory brands.

And that's how I got my first freelance "client," which turned out to be a guy (and what seemed like his ten cats) working from home as a design broker for them.

_____

2. It's since relocated.

You can imagine this relationship wasn't quite set up for success. The communication channels between me and my "handler," and he and the client, were so indirect and hands-off that I often had to track down items myself—the bags, cloths, filters, and even vacuum models—to create 3D mechanical drawings for the products' packaging.

Plus, I was young, naive, and had very little business acumen. Those things are easy to exploit, and he capitalized on all of them to take advantage of my time.

Sure, it was cool to see something I had helped create hanging on a peg at my local Target, but every time I did, I could only think of how frustrating the experience with each project had been and how many unpaid invoices were stacking up. So I did the smart thing for myself and ended that relationship. Luckily, I got paid for all the work I did, but only after I worked up the courage to demand a check for the money I'd earned.

After that, I was ready to move on to the next thing.

It certainly wasn't an ideal experience, and not the last relationship I had with a client that wasn't ideal. But it helped me learn the type of work I valued and how valuable my time was to me.

Be open to anything, and take time to find something you love

With the dry cloud of vacuum cleaner dust behind me, I started to explore many different opportunities. Everything from designing T-shirts to programs for local arts organizations; designing and developing mobile apps and websites to publishing children's books. Of course, some of these experiences I enjoyed more than others, and they all came with various levels of success.

But I found my stride when I started working with entrepreneurs. I got really excited about helping people launch their ideas, and brochure websites (in particular) were a service space that became a niche for me in helping those ideas come to life.[3] For a time, I was the guy in my business circle that could get a quality site up and running in a short time frame, at a reasonable price. And referrals followed each completed project because of the delivery, which often drives value when someone needs a website quickly.

I defined a price and a timeline, and delivered within that expectation. Repeat business came because my clients knew they could trust me to do what I promised, and do it well. But it took a lot of patience to find this niche, and I made a lot of mistakes along the way.

There are two reasons I was able to find and maintain a steady stream of freelance opportunities so that I could keep moving and learning: I got out of my comfort zone and networked, and I took a lot of pride in client satisfaction. That's how I learned the importance of building trust with clients and how that trust can lead to some excellent word-of-mouth advertising.[4]

In fact, I never made a cent off a project that ended up being one of my favorite freelance experiences. I did get a free trip out of it, though. In 2015 I got to work with a team publishing a children's book—the connection made through a mutual contact—who flew me out to work from the Facebook offices in Manhattan for a few days.

It happened to be the right opportunity at the right time. My wife and I had just learned that we were going to have a daughter, and the book's narrative had a very empowering message for young girls.

---

3. Brochure sites are simple websites that outline the products and services a company provides.
4. The best kind, because it's free!

I saw it as an opportunity to have a thing I could show her when she was old enough and say, "Daddy made this for you," so no lack of budget was gonna cause me to turn that one down.[5]

Know when to walk away

After a couple of years working in the industry and building trust with my best clients, most of my freelance prospects grew organically. People happily recommend you to their friends and colleagues when you consistently deliver your promises.

As time passed, the personal value of my freelancing efforts shifted from exploring opportunities and building my portfolio to working with new people and building relationships. Through reflection, I learned that many of my early client relationship failures were my fault; the result of me not yet understanding how to navigate professional relationships, communicate with others about what I do properly, or identify the proper path to establishing trust.

I got better at these things through experience and continued effort.

Honesty and communication of your value and knowledge up-front are the most critical steps in developing trust with any client. But every client is different. People are people, as they say.[6] Some can be difficult to work with, while others seem too good to be true, trusting the value you bring to their project and allowing you the freedom to do it right.

No matter how long you work in this industry, you'll never completely escape situations where you have little control over client expecta-

---

5. This is one of those occasions I talked about where working for free made sense for me.
6. Or, as the wise diner owner in The Muppets Take Manhattan told Kermit: "Peoples is peoples."

tions. Someone will reach out to you about a project, and you'll get the impression that they want to work with you—in particular—only to realize they just want the work done, and done the way they want it.

There's no value in that type of work.

When it comes to design, too many people still see this industry as a trade. They figure that anyone can do the job the way they want it done, and are just looking to hire someone to execute their idea at their direction. All the research and knowledge in the world won't steer them away from the logo they drew on a napkin at 2 a.m. in some bar.

That's just one of many red flags to look out for. Know when to disagree, know when to walk away, and always be honest. Some relationships can be way more valuable than projects, but neither is worth a headache.

Constantly learn and build your expertise, and your brand

When getting started as a freelancer, you have to look at the journey as an opportunity to learn. While your clients may be the expert at their business or industry, it will always fall on you to be the design expert regardless of your experience.[7] And you probably aren't one yet, so this is your time to start down that path.

Why? Because even though our clients can't be the expert at all things, some will undoubtedly try to be.

---

7. Hopefully you become an expert on their business, too.

You have to be able to back up your work and your ideas, or else you're likely going to lose in any power struggle or coin toss when you and your clients don't see eye-to-eye. The more effectively you can communicate your understanding of a problem and work with other people to develop high-performing solutions, the more trust you will build with that person.

Simple things like always meeting deadlines and delivering on promises go a long way toward building that trust and help build something much more valuable: Your brand.

Now, I don't mean your logo or your company name. I mean your reputation; what you become known for by serving and interacting with clients. Nothing starts to break down trust and tarnish your personal brand like constant apologies for being behind on deliverables. And while a breakdown in trust leads to a breakdown in working relationships, your brand can suffer longer-lasting effects.

It's also important to be honest with your branding. If your freelance "company" is just you, and will likely always be you, then don't try to fool people and make yourself seem bigger. I often think about how Aaron Draplin refers to Draplin Design Co. as "we," even though it's mostly just him.[8] No one is confusing you with an agency, so let your skill and passion—not your size—sell your business.

And while we're on that topic, you should also spend the money and get help from a lawyer to create a solid contract. You're building a business for yourself and will often be the sole representative for that business, so take good care of it.

---

8. He's probably earned the right to do that.

Build something for yourself, not exclusively for your clients

Someone recently told me: "You remember 10% of what you read, but 90% of what you teach." That's a strong statement on the power of sharing knowledge, and highlights how we can be better learners by sharing what we know with others.

Today, I'm driven by the idea that we all learn better when we do it together, no matter where that knowledge sharing occurs.

I became interested in design education very early in my career and started working on a master's degree—for the most part—so I could teach. Before taking a hiatus to work on this book, I was lucky to teach at four different universities, from small private schools to large public institutions. Eventually, I started exploring that passion by speaking at conferences and writing about design around the same time that I came to the consulting world.

And now I've found myself in the classroom again as a student.

The similarities become rather apparent when you spend enough time in these worlds—learning, teaching, consulting, and freelancing. My time in consulting, for example, taught me the significant differences between it and the agency world, where I spent the prior portion of my career as a designer. In consulting, I learned how important it is to work with clients rather than for clients. And a focus on human-centered design and working with agile teams showed me the value of making things with people, rather than for people; how to use design to solve problems, rather than to sell products.

These are all simple but critical designations that help me articulate the value I bring to my working relationships today, regardless of whether those relationships exist in a classroom or with a freelance client.

Today, most of my "freelance" work is more consulting than anything. Because I don't have time to design things outside of work and school hours. But I've got plenty of time to talk, though, and seek out mutually-beneficial relationships with people who want to learn and share. That is, as long as those relationships aren't breaking any type of non-compete clause.[9]

Building expertise in something doesn't have a lot of inherent value if you aren't sharing what you know with others.

In particular, I'm always down to answer questions about app development because it's such a big scary thing for someone that has an idea for an app but doesn't know what it takes to make that idea a reality.

One of my colleagues has a setup where he charges people for one-hour meetings (no more) just to answer their questions about creating a new thing—like a brand, a blog, or an app—with no commitment to do that work. It's like a mini Q+A consulting deal.

Initiatives like this—that stress design work is knowledge work, not skilled labor—are significant for our industry and help steer perspectives away from seeing design as a trade skill. Our ideas and expertise provide the real value to any initiative, and people need to understand that our time is just as valuable as the things we create.

---

9. Always read the fine-print and be aware of your employment contracts so you know when it is or isn't ok to work with freelance clients in specific industries, or freelance at all.

Work on, or around, your time. Not theirs.

When I was still freelancing, I didn't have much time to meet with clients face-to-face, and I actually preferred to work with people outside of where I lived.

It was just easier to do the remote thing when physical meetings weren't possible to begin with. Today, most of us have gotten used to working remotely, so this should be an easy arrangement for people on both sides of the relationship.

Regardless of your experience with remote work, make sure to schedule video calls as much as you can and always—always—present your work. Don't send your clients PDFs with bullet point notes on all the things you need to communicate. Don't forward a DropBox link and just say, "here it is."

Schedule time for a thoughtful presentation. And allow your clients to ask questions to avoid miscommunication, or misinterpretation.

Bonus: It's also easier to avoid pro-bono work when you're working remotely and, likely, have no vested interest in your client's community. While I believe in pro-bono work (in certain scenarios) and, on occasion, donate my time for the right cause, I'm still trying to run a business, and my time is valuable.

When kicking off a new client relationship, be honest with them about your other commitments and expected working schedule. Always be upfront with how long something will take and how much effort is required.

As long as you do good work and deliver on time, no one should be concerned about when you work or how long something will take.

I think this is one of the reasons I never had luck freelancing for agencies. Everything always has too much immediacy about it. Usually, if you get a freelance project from an agency, it's because someone realized at the last minute that they weren't going to get it done, so now they're trying to make it your problem.

Do you want to put yourself in stressful situations that cause you to work a 70 hour week just to meet someone else's (likely imaginary) deadline? I don't.

Ultimately, don't be afraid of the idea of freelancing. Just don't expect that it will lead to immediate success. Being your own boss comes with a lot of responsibilities but also allows you to move fast, make mistakes, and learn lessons. That's where the real value lies.

Always start with a sketch

It's the fastest way to turn abstract ideas into concrete solutions

One of my favorite stories is the legend of how James Cameron pitched his idea for *Aliens,* the sequel to Ridley Scott's 1979 film *Alien.* It's a tale I always *hoped* was true until Lynda Obst confirmed its authenticity in her book *Hello, He Lied.*

Even though it grossed over $100 million at the box office—on a measly $11 million budget—*Alien* wasn't seen as a super financial success (it was certainly no *Star Wars*). Still, a sequel opportunity took nearly seven years to develop, which is an unthinkably long gap today. So, coming off the success of 1984's *The Terminator,* James Cameron got a chance to pitch his next project, with an understanding that "Alien 2" was not on the table.

The story goes that he walked into a room full of executives, strolled up to a chalkboard, and wrote the word "ALIEN" in large capital letters.

And the room was quiet.

Then he added an S to the end, and all the suits perked up a little.

Finally, he drew two vertical lines through the S, turned around, and grinned.

Pitch over—dramatic applause. A budget of $18 million was green-lit that day without anyone reading a treatment.

Aside from this being the most incredible movie pitch in the history of movie pitches,[10] I often use this story to illustrate that no matter how complex or straightforward a creative idea is, understanding your audience and what gets them excited is the key to selling it. Bonus points if you can communicate that idea with just a few lines on paper, or marks on a chalkboard.

Proof of concept

Software is often self-serving, and our heavy use of programs trains us to believe that digital tools are all we need to create. Sure, we rely on software for the final execution of most design ideas, and that's unlikely to change.

But computers lack creative, generative power, and they certainly don't allow for quick iteration and exploration the way good, old-fashioned pencil and paper do.[11]

Think about the last thing you worked on—whether it was an ad campaign, a brand refresh, or even a simple icon illustration. There's a good chance you jumped straight from creative brief (or class project outline) to keyboard, relying on the magic computer machine to

---

10. For an example of a really bad one, check out Key & Peele's take on "Gremlins 2" with "The Hollywood Sequel Doctor."
11. Or, sure, marker and whiteboard.

give shape to your idea.[12] We all fall victim to this over-reliance on digital tools from time to time, some of us more often than others.

I have, surprisingly, worked with designers 10–15 years into their journey who resist even simple sketching by hand for planning purposes. So I understand that convincing yourself (or others) to invest time into sketching can be a genuine hurdle.

But when you don't prioritize it as a regular part of your practice you risk leaving a lot of valuable ideas on the table, and limit your growth as a well-rounded storyteller and problem solver. In my experience, analog tools will always provide more value than digital ones when it comes to ideation and iteration.

You may be thinking, "But I can't draw!" Visual thinking and idea generation can succeed even if it's ugly, because sketching is a functional process that doesn't need artistic proficiency. It's so much less about generating art than it is about generating a conversation.

Your work may be good today, but trust me, your process could be significantly improved by starting with a sketch.

Sketching = visual thinking

Take a second to count the number of times you were able to align with a client, professor, or teammate on an idea that existed solely in your brain. It's too easy to get burned by things that only "sound good" on paper. Either someone rejects your idea because they can't visualize it the way you do, or your idea gets misinterpreted

---

12. Here's a story I don't need to tell but is 100% true: Years ago, when I was working at an in-house agency, a student interested in design came in for a studio tour. As she sat with one of my coworkers, he showed her some layout sketches he was working on for a publication, and I shit you not, the following words came out of her mouth: "So you take all of this and put it in the computer, and that makes it look pretty?"

through lack of clarity and that person walks away with an alternative understanding.

When abstract ideas lack concrete presentation: Game over.

That's why I always start with pencil and paper for rapid idea generation and refinement. Whether I'm working with my product development team on a feature or pitching ad campaign concepts to a creative director, it's the first step in testing and validating my ideas. Building on those ideas during the sketching process allows me to explore alternatives quickly, separate strong compositions from weak ones—practical from impractical—and reveal potential issues that don't translate from thought to execution.

When you aren't afraid to table judgment and let the ideas flow in a loose format, you foster an open environment for creative exploration, discussion, and, finally, refinement.[13]

You see, sketches are generally inviting in a way that finished designs can't be. They beg us to challenge them and make them better. Refined digital designs imply effort and confidence and drive feedback on the execution of the idea rather than the idea itself, while marks on paper are disposable, changeable ideas.

If the idea isn't solid, the execution really doesn't matter.

I've often considered explanatory sketching—the ability to quickly convey ideas in a simple way that others can understand—as a necessary skill set for effective creative directors. When the execution of an idea doesn't fall on yourself, you must know how to explain it successfully, or else you'll find yourself having to re-explain.

---

13. And learning, too. Iteration is an incremental process of learning.

Sketching your ideas with others always leads to faster alignment.

But sketching isn't a practice suited only for internal ideation. Olly Moss—famous for his alternative movie poster designs and other pop culture work—employs an ideation process that's heavy on thought, and light on execution, when developing concepts for clients. He says, "I want to pitch you the weird thing. I will send you a sketch that will take me eight hours to think of and five minutes to do."

When you focus on solidifying and simplifying the concept first, it's much easier to communicate it to others in a way they will understand.

Generating discussion

Overall, sketches give us the power to talk about our ideas concretely, and allow others to become invested and provide valuable feedback. The less refined they are, the more commentary they'll likely invite. Loose sketches are perfect for a team's internal dialogue; client-facing sketches call for a higher level of fidelity and refinement.

The practice of sketching goes beyond turning the abstract into the concrete. If you're a product designer, sketching with your team can help outline the big idea, solidify flow, and align agreement on the screens that need to be designed. The latter eliminates surprises when you ultimately turn those sketches into a high-fidelity prototype.[14] All of this, of course, leads to more confident, highly collaborative teams.

The story I opened with may sound like a grand gamble, but behind it lies some pretty simplistic logic: More aliens = more money = happier studio executives. It didn't rely on storyboards or character descrip-

---

14. Or create a paper prototype that allows you to further test that idea before hitting the computer.

tions, just a big idea presented in a few lines of chalk. James Cameron knew what motivated his audience, so he took the approach best-suited to sell his idea.

It may be some time before you find yourself on a studio lot pitching an idea for a film. Until then, approach sketching as a design tool and a tool to facilitate discussion. Practice and keep it simple, and try to develop a routine.

Whether you're kicking off a design sprint or doing research for a brand development, sketching is one of the best logical starting points. Whiteboards and Post-it notes work just fine.[15] My go-to tools are Ticonderoga No. 2 pencils, ultra-fine-tip Sharpies, Field Notes, and Moleskine journals, and I keep them on me at all times.

Not everyone can draw, but anyone can sketch a great solution to a problem. Because there's no tool more adept at creative output than the human brain and body.

15. And if you and your colleagues are remote, there are a lot of great digital products that recreate these tools for virtual collaboration.

Simplicity is a discipline

Even the most complex problems call for simple solutions

Here's a lesson I learned a long time ago from Chip Kidd, the famous book jacket designer: He recalled that—on his first day of design school—his professor walked to the chalkboard and drew a picture of an apple. Then he wrote the word Apple and said: "Listen up. You either say this," pointing to the word Apple, "or you can show this," pointing to the picture of the apple. "But you don't do this," he said, pointing to a picture of an apple with the word Apple beneath it. "Because this is treating your audience like a moron. And they deserve better."[16]

That is a simple but compelling story that draws attention to the importance of clear visual messaging in design.

---

16. You can check this story out for yourself in Kidd's quirky TED talk "Designing books is no laughing matter. OK, it is."

Any seasoned designer should tell you that "simplicity" is an essential aspect of visual communication to achieve that type of clarity. But what do they really mean by this?

Unfortunately, many confuse the term simplicity with "minimalism," which is wholly different. Minimalism is a style; a design concept that relies on simple geometry, negative space, and a limited color scheme.[17]

Simplicity isn't a style but rather a philosophy. While Minimalism focuses on "less," simplicity is about "just enough." Achieving simplicity in a design solution relies on constant refinement to communicate just the right amount of information to articulate your idea clearly. And sometimes—through this process of improvement—more may actually lead to less.

In the first season of Netflix's *Abstract: The Art of Design*, Illustrator Christoph Niemann says, "each idea requires a very specific amount of information." Sometimes it's a lot of detail; sometimes it's just one line or pixel. "But each idea has one moment on that scale."

To further explain this concept, he discusses the process of illustrating a heart icon: "So let's say you want to illustrate the idea of a heart as a symbol for love." At one far end of that scale lies a simple red square: The ultimate abstraction of a heart that no one will understand. It's a solution that lacks the necessary information to communicate the concept.

A realistic human heart made of flesh and blood lies at the other end. With this symbol, Niemann argues that the last thing anyone would think about is "love." But somewhere between the entirely abstract and fully realistic versions of the heart lives the symbol we all know.

---

17. This is an obvious oversimplification, but I don't want to spend unnecessary time defining what this conversation is *not* about.

The one that looks a little bit like both and is "just right to transport this idea of a symbol for love."

Describing this "simplicity scale" highlights how communicating the most complex or straightforward ideas often relies on balancing too much and not enough information. Like Mark Twain famously said: "I didn't have time to write a short letter, so I wrote a long one instead." It takes time and a disciplined working process to achieve the right balance.

Initial ideas are rarely simple

In our last conversation, we talked about the importance of sketching out ideas as a means of refinement. That's because designers often focus on visual problems, with solutions that are creatively visualized through rapid idea generation. And most of us know that initial ideas are usually anything but simple.

The ideation process is where you should be free to let your mind run wild and not yet count anything out as a bad idea, or an unfit solution. But once you've had a chance to reflect, and to refine, those ideas—validating which ones are worthy and which ones are garbage—you want to perfect the "yeses" and the "maybes" into the most powerful solutions possible before taking any one of them to the finish line.

The act of qualifying a design solution is no different than the exercises I went through when writing this book, reviewing and refining each paragraph, each sentence, each word. As early 20th-century French poet Antoine de Saint-Exupery famously said: "Perfection is achieved not when there is nothing more to add, but when there is nothing left to take away."[18]

---

18. John Maeda—former president of the Rhode Island School of Design—gave us a

Designers should never take for granted that they can often communicate a lot with a little. Take Roger Kastel's 1975 poster for the film *Jaws* as an example of perfectly achieved simplicity in visual storytelling.[19]

Most of you can likely picture this image: A nude woman swims in calm water as a great white shark—razor-sharp teeth on display—approaches her from beneath. A simple title in blood-red block letters completes the scene. It's a composition that communicates thematically, tonally, and emotionally with only five visual elements: Woman, shark, water, sky, and title.

Like any good movie poster (or book cover), it tells you exactly what the story is about while also making you want to see (or read) more.

Achieving simplicity requires continuous review

Achieving simplicity of any design solution requires you to follow both a *deductive* and a *reductive* process, reviewing and removing detail and complexities until you've communicated that idea in the simplest way possible, with just the right amount of information.

In visual design, this means letting go of redundant details. When designing a product or service that people will use, it means letting go of redundant steps or processes. If you have to explain to anyone what a finished design solution means, that solution will likely fail.

---

different understanding of the concept when he said: "Simplicity is about subtracting the obvious and adding the meaningful." There are many schools of thought out there. You should explore all of them.
19. His poster was heavily influenced by the original book jacket, which was designed by Paul Bacon—one of the foremost cover illustrators of the 20th century—a year prior.

The story of the redesign of London's Underground Map can teach us a lot about the importance of reducing complexities in design to achieve clarity and usability.

The original map—created in 1908—contained lots of real-world details. Rivers, trees, bodies of water all cluttered the map amongst the train stations. Though it was an authentic representation (from a geographical point of view), it was a mess for passengers to use.

In the early 1930s, English technical draughtsman (and frequent "tube" patron) Henry Charles Beck took a shot at revising the overly detailed map based on a pretty simple theory: Train passengers only needed to know where to get on and where to get off. They didn't care what was happening above ground; they just wanted to get from points A to B.

Beck's redesigned map focused only on stations and routes, simplifying the organic lines of the railways to only three directions: Vertical, horizontal, and diagonal. The result was no longer a 1:1 physical representation of the geographic area and train routes. It wasn't, as we would say, "accurate." But it had something much better going for it: It was a map that people could actually understand—and use—because it eliminated all of the unnecessary information and detail. Today, Beck's map has been in use—and gone virtually unchanged—since its release in 1933.

Eliminating complexities

Simpler designs are often easier for people to use. Especially ones that feel familiar.

That is one of the main reasons Google launched their Material Design system—a visual component library and the guidelines for using it—to help interface designers worldwide design products that people can understand by employing familiarity.[20] Design systems— like Material Design or Apple's Human Interface Guidelines—allow designers to easily pull common elements (and patterns) to design and develop products and experiences, rather than reinventing the wheel with each new design solution. And they are subject to constant review to help them grow and evolve.

The concept of standardizing design libraries isn't new.

The work of German industrial designer Dieter Rams had a profound impact on a generation of designers who, today, value simple aesthetics. Through his work with consumer products company Braun,[21] Rams believed that design's role was to elevate the essential functions of a product, not to overshadow them. At Braun, Rams developed a concise visual language for all of the brand's industrial products that reflected his mantra: "Simplicity is the key to excellence."

Particularly, Rams was troubled by the variety of styles and colors found in most products—designed by his contemporaries—in the 1970s. In "The World of Dieter Rams: Less is More," he recalled the simple decision to color the = button on his famous Braun ET66 Calculator yellow while using black and brown muted tones for the rest of the product design.

"Design should not dominate things, not dominate people," he said. "It should help people." With this simple, restrained design choice, he made the whole product more colorful without actually making the whole product more colorful.[22]

---

20. Material.io/design
21. Pronounced "brown."
22. It's easy to see the influence he had on Jony Ive—Former Chief Design Officer of Apple— in products like the iPhone, the MacBook, etc. Without Dieter Rams, the products we use today would likely look very different (and be more complicated).

Each year, Siegel+Gale publishes The Simplicity Index, a ranking of brands with the least complex experiences, otherwise known as "The World's Simplest Brands." According to their website: "Since 2009, a stock portfolio comprised of the publicly traded simplest brands in our global Top 10 has outperformed the major indexes by 679%."

It's tough to ignore data like that.

The Simplicity Index seeks to showcase that people are more likely to recommend and pay more for brands with uncomplicated experiences. And it's no surprise that people are also more likely to enjoy simpler experiences.

The companies most commonly at the top of The Simplicity Index—Google, Amazon, Netflix, and others—help spotlight how easy-to-use products and services for all result in higher adoption, user satisfaction, and brand loyalty, while also leading to higher performance and a greater return on investment for brands. But the inverse is just as true: Poor and complicated design execution can kill a brand and alienate customers.

Our goal, as designers, should always be to design something that is instantly understood or easily navigable, not leave the viewer or user with more questions. The people that interact with the products, screens, and experiences we design should be able to say instantly, "I get it."[23]

So keep it simple.

---

23. This eureka moment is beautifully illustrated in Steve Krug's book *Don't Make Me Think.*

Worse than being called 'ugly'

How bad design affects bank accounts

In part one, I gave you everything you need to avoid making poor design decisions (and, by extension, poor design). But the impact of bad design goes beyond receiving negative feedback about the look, quality, or user experience. It can be worse than losing clients or straining relationships. For a business, bad design can seriously affect the bottom line.

We're all bound to hear these phrases uttered at some point in our careers: "We can't afford that." "It's not going to fit in the budget." "Can you do it any cheaper?" The people who don't understand the value of design are always concerned about the price tag.

In today's convenience and technology-driven economy, it's frustrating that so many businesses still struggle to justify the expense of design, or treat it like a commodity that warrants bargaining.

Haggle for prices at swap meets, not for the future success of your brand.

As stewards of "good design," it's our responsibility to communicate the actual value of our work and the natural impact design has on revenue. Sure, saving a few dollars may sound good to any budget-conscious business owner, but experienced designers know that a lack of investment in design up-front often leads to paying more for design in the long run. You've got to spend money to make money, as they say.

Even worse, a lack of design investment can result in the loss of a loyal customer base and do a lot of damage to a business's reputation. British-German automotive executive Ralf Speth, the former CEO of Jaguar Land Rover, once said, "If you think good design is expensive, you should look at the cost of bad design."

There are several real-world consequences to neglecting design's role in a business, product, service, or experience. And the effects can extend beyond the pocketbook.

Bad design hurts credibility

Think about all the applications you've downloaded, then deleted because they were too complex to use. According to user growth expert Andrew Chen, more than 75% of users abandon an app within the first 3–7 days of download.[24] That window to create an excellent first impression is super tight. If an app doesn't make good on its promise quickly—and sustainably—it risks losing potential users to competitive applications.

---

24. AndrewChen.com

The same goes for websites. Say you visit a brand's site to learn more about a consumer product they offer, and then find that their website is poorly-organized or offers a broken user experience. Would you have a lot of faith in purchasing one of their products?

On top of that, you're less likely to visit that site again. "I wonder what their competitor is up to?" you'll think.

Culturally, everyone has their own views on what's acceptable as "good design" and what impacts their purchasing decisions. I read a lot of books, so I spend a lot of time in bookstores. Sometimes tracking down titles that were recommended to me by colleagues; the point-of-sale being my first real interaction with the product. Because I'm a generally fastidious person, no glowing recommendation has ever led me to purchase a book with a "cheap" looking cover.[25]

Because of the way I process things, a lack of design effort leads to immediate distrust of whatever content exists inside that book.

That doesn't mean that the secret to a successful book cover is just making it look good. It's about the results you wish to trigger with that book cover, driven by the message you want to communicate.

Your imagination is a lot of things, but it's never wrong

There's no argument movie studios believe that stars sell tickets. But do they always sell merchandise? For example, suppose I wanted to pick up a copy of F. Scott Fitzgerald's *The Great Gatsby* and had to choose between a cover featuring Leonardo DiCaprio and *any other cover*. In that case, I'm going with the non-Leo version every time.

25. Depending on your source, fastidiousness basically means "obsessive about precision" or "difficult to please."

That goes for any property that's made the transition from literature to screen.

Now I'm not saying that this version of the book is a bad design, but when marketing to bibliophiles across the world, it's a bad design decision. Of course, I know the movie is based on the book. But I don't want the film influencing my reading experience, goddammit!

When I sit down to read, I want the chance to form my own opinion of how the characters look in my head. It's an important part of the experience that I'm robbed of when I see Leo every time I pick it up. Sure, many people probably bought that version of the book, but a lot probably didn't buy it as well.

There's always a chance that the smallest design decision can alienate customers.

The point is: Design begins with research. Understanding the market, the competition, and the audience. The logical outcomes of that research influence our design decisions. The coolest design will fail if it doesn't speak to the audience, align with the brand promise, or establish trust with the customer.

Design has an emotional impact

We build more human-to-digital experiences every day, and the products we interact with should make our lives easier, not more difficult. We particularly expect technology to provide a sustained positive impact, and certainly not lead to frustration. But that isn't always the outcome.

Aside from low adoption—or quick deletion—bad design can impact the user emotionally. In the early days of mobile technology, it was more common for someone to assume user error when faced with a product they couldn't understand. "I must not be smart enough to figure this out" is easier to pass off when we're all figuring something out together.

Today's consumer is very picky and expects a positive experience from end-to-end, surface-to-core. They have every right to this expectation, and our job is to understand it and make it happen.

And plan how to handle it when it fails.

If an experience leaves someone with negative emotions, the whole world is likely to hear about it on various social media platforms. Those types of stories travel fast and lead to a negative impact on a brand's credibility and public image.

While it can be argued that we were once more accepting of bad design, today we're just emotionally drained by it. Poor experiences zap our energy and enthusiasm.

As a designer, it's ok to be bothered by products and services you interact with when they aren't perfect, as long as you turn that into a desire to fix it. And I have a great, personal example to illustrate that idea.

Over the last decade, I've accompanied my wife on a long healthcare journey that's included many bad and broken experiences. Luckily, many opportunities have presented for me to turn those negative encounters into a catalyst for change.

In recent years, I've used design thinking and service design to build better services for several healthcare organizations. I've leveraged design to enable contact centers to retrieve provider and patient information quicker and to standardize processes that allow health networks to address broken moments of trust with patients more comprehensively. Mid-pandemic, I used customer experience research to help a national pharmacy chain scale public access to COVID-19 information, tests, and vaccines.

And now, I run a product design team for a health tech company, using design to deliver care to patients in the convenience economy.

Through all of these efforts, I was able to turn our negative experiences into a passion for change, delivered through design. The ability to use design for positive impact is one of the reasons I love what I do, with no intent ever to stop.

Bad design impacts brand loyalty

Many people don't make purchasing choices in sensible ways. Factors like quality, perceived value, and lifestyle fit often outweigh the cost of a product when alternatives exist. Don't believe me? How often do you drop $10 on a cup of coffee at Starbucks?

Our emotional reaction to products is a driving force behind purchasing them. Take the emotion out of the equation, and there's no practical reason anyone would spend thousands of dollars on handbags and watches other than their ability to.

This phenomenon is called "brand loyalty," and it's the reason major brands spend billions of advertising dollars every year. Consumer product and service choices don't always come down to what's more aesthetically pleasing or even what works better. Most often, it's about how using the product or interacting with the service makes the person feel.

In today's world, an electronically-controlled refrigerator isn't a status symbol. For many, it's a necessity. Telling someone to purchase one without an ice maker or water dispenser is akin to saying they don't need a vehicle with heated seats. You understand that you don't need those features, but you can't imagine life without them once you have them.

Want to guess the average lifespan of one of these newly manufactured refrigerators today? Seven years.[26] Why? Because appliance brands think we expect digital interfaces, voice-control, and touch-screen technology on everything.[27] And they're so eager to give it to us that they don't take the proper time and steps to test thoroughly and vet their products.[28]

Unfortunately, this can be said for most modern appliances: Ovens, microwaves, dishwashers, televisions. The point is, when that poorly-designed product breaks, the owner isn't only looking for a new device, they're most likely looking for a new brand.

Brands live and die by their customers

At the beginning of this conversation, I said that bad design can impact a business beyond just dollars and cents. Poorly designed experiences can lead to broken trust. Poorly designed products can lead to a loss of brand loyalty. Poorly designed services can leave customers looking for a new service provider.

And any of these outcomes lead to a lot of lost revenue.

Don Norman proposed that our emotional system consists of three different yet connected levels that influence our perception of experience: **The Visceral** (our response to the visual qualities of a product), **The Behavioral** (pleasure derived from use), and **The Reflective** (self-image and satisfaction). It's not all about the look or the features.

---

26. According to the guy that just dropped off my new refrigerator.
27. Cheap wine tastes better in fancy glasses, as they say.
28. Where's my proof? I own two 1940s Frigidaires that were purchased brand new by my great grandfather. They run like tanks and haven't been serviced once.

By investing in design at all levels of a company, it's easier to build products and services that delightfully meet user needs, build a personal relationship, and are trustworthy in both quality and visual appeal. Capturing customers at all three levels leads to brand loyalty.

At the end of the day, brands live and die by their customers. When they feel isolated by bad experiences, they likely won't be back for a repeat. That's when the cash flow, and the business, start to dry up.

Bad design creates innumerable problems for brands, but good design always leads to a solid return on investment.

More right than wrong

Design solutions are not a matter of black-and-white

Every agency, organization, and individual has their own approach to validating design solutions during the concept stage. A seasoned designer may rely on a combination of experience, self-validation, and a research-based process to narrow down and refine a single concept. Others may employ an artifact-heavy, rapid creation process that yields many work-in-progress designs that can be socialized and discussed to separate strong solutions from weak ones.

Neither approach is necessarily more right than the other. And as you build expertise, work for different types of clients, and tackle different types of problems, your working process could undoubtedly ebb and flow. I used to lean heavily on the latter between the two descriptions above, while I mostly do the former today.

It was during those artifact-heavy process days of my early-to-mid career that I often found myself having a lot of arguments about which concepts I was developing were "right" and which were "wrong."

Because design can be such a subjective and divisive subject for many people, sharing ideas and working concepts with others can lead to a lot of disagreement. The more people who look at something, the more varied opinions you're likely to receive. And taking all of that feedback into consideration during the concept phase can kill even the best ideas, leading to a compromised design that will not work for anyone.

Separating the weak from the strong

Designers should always consider varied and different directions to solve any design problem. It's a natural part of the process. And constant review and iteration of all ideas are often how valuable solutions are discovered.

But the belief that you can separate early design concepts into right and wrong is, frankly, just wrong. Design isn't a matter of black-and-white. Not so cut and dry.

That was a constant battle between my creative director and myself in a previous role. It was wrong if a potential solution didn't align with their ideas, and it was wrong if the execution wasn't the way they would have done it.

This argument wasn't a matter of pride for me, per se. I wasn't defending the work because I was too attached to it. I just disagreed with the idea that somehow my half-formed, there's-something-there-but-I-just-haven't-cracked-it-yet idea was fit for the recycle bin so soon.[29]

---

29. I always say that you shouldn't work with someone you can't argue with, so make sure you keep those arguments respectful.

So I often found myself responding, something to the flavor of: "I agree that there are other possible solutions, and let's work together until we find something we can both agree on."

Typically, there will be many possible and valuable solutions to any problem. All design ideas will have their strengths and weaknesses, and they can leapfrog one another over and over as you continue to work on them. It's your job to understand which designs work and which designs *need* work throughout the lifecycle of the creative process. Even a weak design solution can become a strong contender through iteration and refinement.

Embracing the randomness

One of my favorite quotes comes from the early Kurt Vonnegut novel *The Sirens of Titan*. The story itself deals with themes of omniscience, purpose, and free will, all of which are summed up—in the third act, by the protagonist—with a single statement: "I was a victim of a series of accidents, as are we all."

It's a tidy little comment about the randomness of life that exists in pretty much everything, even design.

Today, whenever I complete a project—a logo, an interface design, or anything else—I'm usually confident that I've created a successful solution to the stated design problem. Because it's been informed by research and, most likely, validated through user testing. But I also know that if I'd started working on it twenty-four hours earlier, or twenty-four hours later, it could have ended up looking wildly different.

And I embrace that randomness. It's why I often find myself hovering between the incubation and illumination phases of the creative process for as long as I can, knowing that if I start too soon, I could miss out on making a special connection to a piece of inspiration that would significantly change my approach.[30]

Every design solution, produced by any designer, is a result of the time and space they were in when the real work of bringing the idea to life began. Start on it a month later, and it could have gone in thirty different directions, with each potentially being a solid solution to the design problem in its own way.

Yes, that work would still be heavily fed through experience and process, but you can't deny that timing has a little bit to do with it as well.

Resolving disputes with data

Rather than separating right from wrong, focus your design reviews on uncoupling weak from strong. If you still think there's some value in those more fragile ideas, then you better figure out how to shore it up. If not, it's trash can time.

Take what's left and put them to the test. Testing multiple designs early can provide more valuable information than testing a single solution. If you're working on an interface design, try some qualitative, comparative usability testing to assess the pros and cons of each. This way, you'll understand which designs are easy to use and which cause frustration.

If you're working on a consumer package, conduct a survey to understand how people perceive the brand value and market position. If the results don't align with your hypothesis, you know there's a gap between your design solution and the brand promise of that product.

---

30. I cover the four stages of creative thought in "Mom, where do ideas come from?"

When all is said and done, you can use the data from those tests to settle any disagreements about the successful design, rather than arguing about which is right and wrong.[31]

Design can play many roles. Often, it has to connect with someone emotionally, streamline a process, or help someone complete a task in a fulfilling way. There are often many right ways to do that, and very few wrong.

By testing all the solutions you have confidence in, you have actionable data to help you make more informed decisions about the next steps, revisions, and getting that final solution ready for its big date with the client, or the consumer.

---

31. Don't mistake this for advice that you should let data make design decisions for you. Those designs you are testing were built on creative reasoning.

Stop asking for approval

Instead, lean on your expertise to build support

Most designers never seem to agree on one topic of discussion: How to best present work to a client or group of stakeholders. Some prefer to start with mood boards[32] full of inspiration and research, talk about color palette choices and the associations those colors will communicate to customers, or even lead with consumer research data to help clients understand the strategic value in the decisions made.

None of these approaches are necessarily better than any other.

However, the question that leads to the most debate is often: "How many design solutions do I present?" Typically, clients are used to being presented with options to either choose from or provide input on—especially when it comes to brand identities. The benefactor expects their fingerprints to be on the work, so to say.

---

32. A visual collage that communicates the general idea of a design direction. In my opinion, client's don't give two shits about your mood boards.

Shopping options often, and unfortunately, leads to a quantity over quality problem that places weak design solutions in front of people to fill an expected—or unspoken—quota.

If you hold yourself or your teams to one of these ideals, like the "always present three options" methodology: Have you ever presented three options you genuinely have equal confidence in? Three options you've put equal time and energy into? Probably not.[33]

It's more likely that you've spent your time focused on the strongest solution, and neglected the others, with the intent of stacking the presentation in your favor; fingers crossed that everyone will hear you out and make the "right choice."

The practice of placing design in the hands of a client for selection and approval needs to stop because it creates an impression that our work is open to subjective review. Or that design artifacts are nothing more than pieces of art for others to judge and validate. Unfortunately, it's a problem that we created and have enabled for too long. It's time to hold us accountable.

I've certainly been guilty of it myself: Presenting multiple design options to a client, discussing each one's strengths and weaknesses, going deep on the inspiration and the story each can tell, and then leaving the final decision to the client. But this scenario is only ideal if your client knows how to view design objectively. That's a trait that most outside of our profession don't possess, so it often returns unfavorable results.

---

33. Not to mention that you are likely pitting multiple designers against one another to churn out these design options, which means you are wasting some of your own time and resources.

And if you're extraordinarily unlucky, the outcome of this "take your pick" approach leads to review by a committee. Nothing will zap your energy like hearing, "we took a vote, and..."

Likely, that pollster sees shopping designs around the office as a way to get more people invested in the process. But should you—or anyone—care what Sheila in Accounting thinks about the logo directions for the company's new product line?

Most often, however, it just leads to the Frankenstein effect: Multiple people like aspects of various options, so you're now tasked with figuring out how to take parts from some and combine them with others. All that does is undermine the solution, the research that went into it, and your expertise as a designer.

Ditch the options

Several years ago, I took an approach that was common with consumer package design—conducting surveys to assess consumer sentiment—and began applying it to my brand design work. I thought I'd cracked this whole design presentation format wide open once I was able to present three logo options and explain how people described their expectations of the brand value based on each. I was able to say something like, "If you want to lean heavily into your American-made brand promise, then option two is most likely to communicate that value to consumers."[34]

The goal was to redirect the way clients reviewed and evaluated the design options I was presenting, moving away from aesthetic judgment and personal preference-based decisions and toward strategic business decisions. It made sense at the time.

---

34. Assuming this is aligned with one of the business pillars.

But to be honest: I was still doing it wrong.

In 1986 Steve Jobs hired design legend Paul Rand to create the visual identity for NeXT, the computer company he founded after leaving Apple the prior year. During an interview in '93, when asked about what it was like to work with Rand, Jobs recounted, "I asked him if he would come up with a few options, and he said, 'No, I will solve your problem for you and you will pay me. You don't have to use the solution. If you want options, go talk to other people.'"

When you think about it, it's pretty clear that this is the right attitude and the type of courage—and confidence—we need when making design decisions. Paul Rand wasn't concerned with Steve Jobs' approval, and he didn't need it because he was an expert at what he did. His goal was to design a solution that worked, whether his client liked it or not.

In his book *Articulating Design Decisions,* Tom Greever wrote, "the difference between a good designer and a great designer is in their ability to not only solve problems with a design, but to also articulate how their solution solves it in a way that's compelling, fosters agreement, and gets the support needed to move forward."

And that's just it: Why should the people who hire us, or sponsor our work, have to make decisions for us? Why give them the job of telling us how to do ours?

When presenting design solutions, we shouldn't spend time preparing for feedback and revisions. We should focus on communicating our knowledge of the problem and our confidence in the validated solution, then guiding the conversation toward a place of shared understanding and agreement.

Great designers should be great at communicating about design, confidently. Aren't you the expert, after all?

People hire us to do design work because they can't do it themselves. As long as you create an environment where your clients or stakeholders can trust your expertise and have insight into your process, they will learn to value and trust both.

Bring other people into the process

When you ask *anyone* to give their opinion, they'll feel socially obligated to give it to you. That's probably a fact. But the whole reason you're working on a design solution—to begin with—is to help someone else achieve a goal. To build a solution for them that could be successful, not one that they will like.

Most clients don't know how to give feedback, and coaching them on what to say—and how to see—shouldn't be a top priority when developing a new relationship. So asking them for an opinion on the spot will only lead to an impulsive response. It's a clear "you get what you ask for" situation.

Today, I encourage my teams to align on the following goals when presenting informed design solutions: Instead of asking for approval, we ask for support. Instead of seeking sign-off, we seek buy-in.[35] This approach helps keep everyone focused on the fact that we're solving a problem, and we're doing it together.

As long as your client didn't choose you because you were the cheapest option, they should already be expecting good work when you

---

35. Factual approvals—checking for errors, legal copy, shipping details—will always be necessary. And important. If you are prone to errors in your work, it will affect the trust your client has in you.

present it. All you need to do now is explain why you made the decisions you did and how your design solution will solve their problem. The presentation's success depends on your ability to build support from everyone in the room.

It's your responsibility to make sure everyone sees the value you're bringing to the table and get them excited about the solution you're building together.

If you want to make this path even more straightforward, give everyone a look behind the scenes early in the process so they understand how you work. Keep them abreast of research findings, ask questions along the way, and provide insight into the considerations you're working through to keep them feeling involved throughout the project lifespan.

Spend time workshopping problems together. Involving your clients in the ideation phase is always a good idea, and leads to a greater understanding of the problem and path to solution for both parties. Ideas developed collaboratively are far superior to any produced independently.

When you bring external clients along for the ride, you build design advocates within their organization that often lead to long-term relationships.

These people are your partners, after all. To help facilitate equal trust, they need to understand that both sides are on this journey together; that you're working with them, not for them.

Give these ideas a shot, and you'll feel way more confident presenting a single design solution when the time comes. And because you're focused on a single solution, you'll likely be able to develop it to a higher standard and provide a tighter, more focused presentation.

If someone has feedback, you'll know it's coming from an informed perspective. And you'll be able to discuss and distill that feedback to strengthen your design.

Lorem Ipsum is a joke

Why designers should also write

You'll spend countless hours honing new skills that can help you be a more intelligent or versatile designer throughout your career. You may turn your photography hobby into a side hustle, spend your free time on Skillshare learning a new interface design program, or pick up Jessica Hische's excellent book *In Progress* because you want to get better at custom lettering. You may even spend so much time talking about design or the skills you've picked up that you start sharing what you've learned with others on an open-source platform like Medium.[36]

There are tons of bonus skills to chase, all valuable to designers in different ways. But we rarely talk about writing as a design skill.

In our day-to-day, we laboriously push pixels, carefully choose and place visual elements intended to connect emotionally with our audience, or obsess over the steps and dependencies of a process to

---

36. That's where I started perfecting my writing voice before working on this book.

provide a user with a better experience. And we do these things with a passion because we love it.

I think it's really important we learn to do the same with words. As the people at 37Signals wrote in their eBook *Getting Real:* "If you think every pixel, every icon, every typeface matters, then you also need to believe every letter matters."

Content and design go hand-in-hand

Excellent writing ensures that content is informative and easy to understand. In the same way good content leads to clear messages in print communications, it has the same crucial impact on effortless user experiences. Words should be just as carefully chosen as a color palette or an icon style in all design efforts.

Ignoring copy in the early design stages only delays the focus on solving a problem, hoping that someone else will worry about it later.

For a long time, using the placeholder text Lorem Ipsum[37] has been a widely accepted solution for designers looking to make early progress on a design when a client or copywriter said: "I'd like to see the design first. Go ahead and get started, and I'll provide copy later."

We've all had someone suggest "just grab some Lorem Ipsum" at one time or another when we needed to fill out a layout template or test typeface combinations. But how often did those decisions turn into something useful? More likely, you had to adjust your layouts or font choices once you received that copy.

Let's be honest: Using filler text is a lazy practice. Relying on the approach treats valuable context as an afterthought rather than an

---

37. Also known as "dummy text."

equally important element in an overall design strategy. Every text passage represents your brand voice, or allows someone to use your product successfully, or helps someone make sense of important data. Whatever role copy plays—no matter how small—it's always important.

While placeholder text may seem an easy solution, using it can do more harm than good. Even if you have every intention of replacing it down the road.

The real value of dumb copy

Regardless of all the origin stories you can find online, Lorem Ipsum is nothing more than nonsensical Latin text. It became famous as a time-saver method to help us imagine the complete visual form of an in-progress design. It's the antithesis of meaningful content: It has no substance, no message, no value beyond being slightly better than a blank page.

Its existence is problematic because visuals and words go hand-in-hand to create valuable design solutions. Isolating content from design—at any phase of the process—can result in a disconnected strategy, misunderstanding of intent, and poor communication of an intended design solution.[38] Even worse, that placeholder Lorem Ipsum could go live, leading to embarrassing situations for brands.

As a practice, it's inefficient for communicating about design solutions because it only leads to unrealistic interpretations. How are you supposed to collaborate with your teammates or clients using gibberish? When building a design solution, you not only have to focus on

38. For those of you who use Lorem Ipsum as a go-to time saver: It will often lead to heavy redesign. Good luck finding the time.

the visual form and organization of the content or the message that content communicates, but you've also got to think about the people who need to interpret your design work.

People are drawn to text. If you put words in front of someone, they will read them. If that content is nonsense, they're going to be confused. Not just about the words, but the intended audience for the design solution and its role in solving a problem for them.

It's also near impossible to get valuable feedback on something that uses placeholder copy. It's like watching a television show in a foreign language. You may think you understand it, but you wouldn't bet money on it.

Thanks to more brilliant, strategy-focused designers, using Lorem Ipsum is becoming an outdated convention. Instead, designers are putting on their journalist hats[39] and taking an empathetic or research-based approach to copy, even if it's a placeholder.

Turning dumb copy into smart copy

Instead of filling in the blanks later, research competitor content to give yourself a logical starting point to connect messaging to intent. Or, better yet, think about the message that needs to be communicated and put yourself in the shoes of the person you're speaking to—or designing for—to make more logical choices that connect visuals and copy.

And then drop in some damn copy.

If you haven't figured it out by now, every skill you add to your professional tool belt will help set you up to be a better, more versatile, more

---

39. The ones with the little press passes sticking out of them.

in-demand problem solver. And writing should be at the top of your list for its power in helping you grow and influencing the way you think.

Because the parallels between text and visuals are most potent when it comes to building context, understanding how to write well will make you a better communicator and storyteller. After all, design *is* a form of visual storytelling.

Like writers, great designers should understand their audience. So you should be smart enough to know that if a person can't read something, they can't understand it. If they can't understand it, it's also likely they can't use it or benefit from it. So instead of using thoughtless text at any point of the design journey, stay focused on what your design solution is trying to accomplish and distill that into words that your intended audience—or user—can understand.

Don't worry; I'm not encouraging you to write the final copy. If it's easier for you, consider it a rough draft. It just needs to make sense— using a tone and voice that captures the intent of the "final" copy—to help everyone who interacts with it, understand it.

Like anything else, the more you do it, the better you'll get.

You can't do that with Lorem Ipsum or any of its offshoots.[40] Excellent writing and great design go hand-in-hand, so the earlier you incorporate writing into your toolset and process, the closer you move toward becoming a more complete designer.

Words are powerful. So are images. Bringing the two together helps you craft effective solutions and clearly communicate them. And contributing to efforts outside of your design expertise makes you a more valuable teammate.

---

40. Hillbilly Ipsum, anyone?

Design is a team sport

How to build high-performing working relationships

I've been lucky to work for organizations that place a high value on collaboration and teaming. Sometimes that's meant working with trusted collaborators for short-term, quick wins, or even longer-term strategy development. And other times, forming new relationships from scratch.

Regardless of the scenario, years of working with others have taught me that I value two things above most: Good work worth doing and the people I do it with.

The key to bringing those two passions together is collaboration. Collaboration fosters our unique ability to perform as a team of individuals contributing to valuable solutions, and supports getting shit done to a high degree. It's the secret sauce for setting teammates, clients, and stakeholders up for immediate and continued success.

I'm not ignoring that some of you may be sole contributors; a team of one. I've been there, too, and understand that pain. So I also know you have plenty of valuable business relationships that need nurturing. Whether you're a team of many or one, you should strive to build similar high-trust working relationships with clients and stakeholders because they're part of your team also. And you're working side-by-side on shared objectives.

Today, I lead a team designing technology-based, human-centered solutions for consumers and service providers; the people who will use the products that the team is creating. But I've also been a member of those product development teams and found myself face-to-face with solving those users' needs.

When looking at real-world problems, the first goal is always to build a thorough understanding. So I empower my teams to ask a lot of probing questions to comprehend what problem we're solving fully. Collaborating with teammates—individuals from different disciplines with different responsibilities and perspectives—is how the answers to those questions are validated. How we can move past assumptions together.

The ability to do this with the people *you* work with is supported by understanding what each person brings to the table, what they value, and how you can best work together. When all members of a team are aligned, good collaboration allows you to utilize the experience, skills, and knowledge of everyone involved.

Building high-trust, collaborative relationships doesn't take magic, or even luck. To do it well, you just have to keep it simple: Be honest and reasonable, foster encouragement, create a safe space that facilitates feedback and accountability, and always give credit where credit is due.

Be honest

Forming as a team, coming together to build new relationships and align on goals is often a difficult task. Especially for the introverted-type designer. The process forces you to be open and honest, which may be challenging for some, or even most. But during team formation, you must bring to the table who you are and what you need so the team can actively work on building trust, and consciously create a common ground so collaboration can begin.

So I think it's essential to start by soliciting ideas and opinions when kicking off new working relationships. I want to understand each person's strengths, interests, and goals—so I know how and when to leverage them—but I also want to make sure everyone has a voice during this process. And I think you should, too.

The act of facilitating multiple points of view early while providing honest input on your needs and goals will aid in the long-term engagement of each team member, which helps cultivate a collaborative environment.

And I've found that no matter if you're building relationships with teammates, clients, or other external or internal partners, honesty is key to facilitating trust. It's also one of the quickest ways to form a relationship with someone.

Even though people are often fearful of it, everyone appreciates honesty. So, if you disagree with a teammate or a client on something, let them know, in a respectful way, of course. When you get someone to understand your point of view and value your opinion, they will keep asking for it.

Be reasonable

When coming together with collaborators, it's important to assess each person's values, so you know when and how to keep people informed. Who needs or wants to know about decisions and changes? Who do those changes affect most? Who doesn't care?

That's why I love team working agreements, because they help set expectations right off the bat. We all have boundaries and other things we're trying to balance, and working contracts help alleviate any misunderstandings.

Team agreements help develop a sense of shared responsibility, increase awareness, and enhance the quality of collaboration by establishing a team culture that empowers total investment from everyone involved in the process.

Also, don't make promises to anyone that you can't keep. Otherwise, the foundation you're trying to build will start to crack, and your teammates will think you're an insincere jackass.

When I moved from the creative agency world that focused on the individual, to the world of agile product development that values the team dynamic, I learned the power of weighing decisions based on their value to the team just as much as their value to the business. Why? Because the slickest design solution will fail if it's not technically feasible for the team to execute. Collaborative team discussions uncover problems like that before it's too late.

Encourage and inspire others

In my opinion, the ideal teammate cares. They're someone who truly wants to understand the value of the thing they are doing or the problem they are solving and encourage others to see that value as well. Hero teammates are the ones that inspire us to be better.

I think that's why I find satisfaction in joining teams that are already chipping away at in-progress work. Being put into a situation where I can come in and say, "tell me what you need," and start to alleviate pains and provide value immediately is when I really feel like I'm making an impact.

That becomes my priority if I find myself with an opportunity to make someone's job easier or help find a new solution to something they're stuck on. I get energized by that instant gratification. That's something you miss out on when everyone initiates a new effort together.

When describing ideal collaborators, I still rely on the concept of the T-shape: Someone with many capabilities that is an expert in at least one. Today, we often hear terms like Versatilist, Wedge-shaped, or Polymath to describe the type of expert that can adapt to varying demands. But I hold to my use of T-shaped for a good reason.

When you consider the legs of the T as deep expertise, and the arms of the T represent broad interests, those who can teach from their legs broaden the reach of others' arms. And when you're able to learn from others with the same deep expertise as yourself, it makes your legs stronger.[41] To me, that's the true embodiment of collaboration: Learning better, together.

---

41. My definition of T-shaped comes from Matt Wallaert's fantastic book *Start at the End: How to Build Products that Create Change.*

Create a safe space

Every person has different, legitimate needs that need to be recognized. Some of your teammates will have great ideas but may not be great communicators. Some people only want to share their honest opinion in a safe space. Others have no problem being pulled into a meeting when their perspective is needed and don't mind when you put them on the spot. And so on.

It's every team member's responsibility to create that space and respect those differences.

I think this is one of the hidden values of agile ceremonies.[42] Group activities like estimating design or development stories give everyone an open forum to share their concerns. Splitting up work during a sprint planning session provides each individual with the opportunity to advocate for the work they want to do—what they're comfortable tackling—at their own pace. And sprint retros allow your team to discuss what's working well and what isn't in an open environment, with a focus on applauding the good and seeking to correct the bad.

Giving each team member ownership over their day-to-day provides people with comfort in their role and the feeling of a job worth doing. But, of course, when someone overcommits or needs help, they have a team backing them up. That's the beauty of having collaborators to lean on.

---

42. Regular occurring meetings that provide a framework for teams to get work done in a structured manner, and empower collaboration.

Hold others accountable (and hope they do the same with you)

Once you understand everyone's personal goals—and know how to leverage strengths and compensate for weaknesses—it's time to find opportunities to advocate for them. Especially, but not limited to, if you find yourself in a leadership position in that environment.[43]

In collaborative conditions, it's ok to push people outside their comfort zones when the opportunity is right. Especially if you know that opportunity is a growing edge for them. If you've built a trusting, collaborative relationship with your teammates, they are more likely to understand that you're trying to help them feel empowered.

When faced with designing a solution for a feature or whatever, a typical exercise that I like to conduct with teammates is to bring documentation to the table and collaborate on potential solutions. Here's the problem we're trying to solve, and here are three ways we can solve it: Let's discuss. This approach gets everyone invested in the solution and leads to faster results.

Plus, it holds everyone accountable for executing that solution and fosters trust with clients and stakeholders when they see that the whole team is on the same page.

As a designer, I don't believe in committing a team of developers to build a thing without their input. And that responsibility runs in both directions. All voices—design, technical, and business expertise—need to inform a solution.

In the product world, we're often trying to answer three questions to determine if something is viable: Does this support the business? Do

---

43. If you aren't, you should still act as an advocate leader.

the users want it? Can we build it? The first two don't mean anything if the answer to the last one is "no."

Receive feedback well and know how to give it

Organizations that place a high value on feedback and provide coaching on both giving and taking it—positive and negative—are becoming more commonplace these days. Because it's important that, throughout the lifespan of a team or even project, everyone stays consistently aligned to goals.

If collaboration starts to break down within your team, you have to take the time to step back and level set on those goals. And part of an honest environment is being honest when things aren't going well or when someone is performing under expectations, so you can focus on how to fix the problem.

Fear exists on both sides, and both parties need to face that fear head-on.

Often, the scariest scenarios are the relationships that begin to break down with clients. When those relationships become strained, it never hurts to remind your client, "Hey, we're here to make you successful. We've got your back because it's our job to make you look good."

We're all on the same team, so it's good to remind people that we're all here to support one another.

Give credit. And do it publicly.

This one is simple: You have to show people appreciation and not expect it in return.

And on the other hand, if you are wrong: Own up to it.

The real point to all of this advice is that collaboration is way more than just you doing your job. It's doing your job in the context of an ecosystem of people. It's supporting one another so that you can better support your clients and your users. It's building trust with someone else so that they trust you.

Otherwise, working together day in and day out isn't gonna be much fun.

When working against a problem, many voices get results. But those voices have to be aligned and in sync. When you take the time to build solid collaboration efforts with everyone involved, problems don't seem so big when everyone is facing them together.

Great things don't happen in silos, but high-performing teams are capable of some cool shit.

Mom, where do ideas come from?

A psychological approach to the creative process

Here's a question I get asked a lot: "Where does inspiration come from?"

It's difficult to nail down inspiration for any project or idea to a single source. Inspiration can strike at any time, as they say. But it can also come from any thing. Creature designer Phil Tippett envisioned a cross between a bear and potato when designing the Rancor: The beast that tries to eat Luke Skywalker in *Return of the Jedi*.[44] That's a pretty wild combo.

Garbage Pail Kids trading cards—once a relic of my childhood, now in vogue once again—was created solely as an attempt to parody

---

44. He also claims to have been on LSD at the time.

Cabbage Patch Kids, the hottest toy line of the time. That one's way more obvious.

But how do people generally get from point A to point B? Or, when inspiration seems a little more random, from point A to point J?

Approaching any new problem presents, in itself, new challenges. If you happen to be tackling that problem in an unfamiliar medium or an emerging industry, even more so. Through trial and error—both conscious and subconscious—all creative people work toward finding solutions to these challenges.

But that doesn't mean we all do it the same way.

Give ten designers carte blanche and wi-fi access to tackle the same design brief, and you'll end up with, likely, ten different solutions. Some might echo the latest industry trends, and others may be heavily influenced by research into the client's business and competition. A few might leave you wondering, "what the fuck were they thinking?"

But all will be reflective of each designer's personal approach to the creative process.

That's the beauty of inspiration: It hits everyone a little differently, and it's usually very personal. One person's process can be messy and disorganized, while others can be purely scientific. For some, the process *itself* is what leads to inspiration.[45]

Regardless of your approach, inspiration isn't something you wait for. Because all the great ideas are already out there. As a creative problem solver, you've got to be hungry enough to go out and find them. Why? Because the personal creative process is often influ-

---

45. The creative folks at House Industries wrote a fantastic book on what inspires them, fittingly titled *The Process is the Inspiration*.

enced more by the things you do outside of work than by the things you do during working hours.

Ideas are like babies

In the forward to *The Creative Process Illustrated*,[46] author and speaker Sally Hogshead wrote: "No one knows exactly when a baby will be born. We can estimate a due date. We can peer in and predict. We can measure this and monitor that. Yet, with all the technological devices and medical advances, birth is still very much the domain of art, not science.

"We don't decide when babies will be born. Babies do."

In all my years working in this field, I've found no better explanation of the messy, chaotic, and laborious process that leads to the birth of ideas.[47] Neither comes from just thin air. Creativity is often fueled by letting your mind wander to see what crazy connections it can make. Usually, the real work happens well before a problem presents itself.

About creativity, Steve Jobs said in a 1996 interview with *Wired*, "Creativity is just connecting things. When you ask creative people how they did something, they feel a little guilty because they didn't really *do* it, they just *saw* something. It seemed obvious to them after a while. That's because they were able to connect experiences they've had and synthesize new things. And the reason they were able to do that was that they've had more experiences or they have thought more about their experiences than other people."[48]

---

46. A book that explores how "advertising's big ideas are born" by Glenn Griffin and Deborah Morrison.
47. See what I did?
48. Do yourself a favor and look up the story of Archimedes and the King's Crown (also known as Archimedes and the Bathtub). Same logic, and also the birth of the "eureka moment."

In my opinion, the creative process is ever in perpetual motion. It begins by soaking up the world around you. Every time you consume literature, music, or art, you add to your internal database of media and culture; filling up your head with fuel for the next creative spark.

Every time you analyze the details of a process, question how something works, or just observe people, you collect data and strengthen your understanding of the world around you. Not to find a solution to a problem you're focused on at the time. You probably do it because you're just a curious person.

A curious mind is a creative mind, and a creative mind can lead to radical ideas. Like Bill Bowerman creating the first pair of Nike sneakers in his home kitchen on a waffle iron. Or moonshot ideas like self-driving cars or landing a man on the Moon.[49] This type of free, experimental thinking leads to significant outcomes.

If you like to solve problems at work and at home, this is a creative process you have likely already embraced. Your creative mind is always working on the solution to something. You may just not know it (yet).

The art of thought

British social psychologist Graham Wallas proposed the first significant model of the "natural thought process" of creativity in his 1926 book *The Art of Thought*. And nearly 100 years later, it's still one of the most widespread theories on creative thinking, outlined as a series of four stages.

The first stage is where you gather information. That usually happens after you first encounter—or begin to understand—a new design

---

49. And now the creators of self-driving cars are sending *themselves* to the Moon!

problem and while you're researching potential solutions. Wallas called this stage **Preparation**. While your conscious mind is considering the task at hand and gathering resources, your subconscious mind is being provoked into making connections. You are digging into that complex database of memories and experiences you've built during work hours and free time.

Next comes **Incubation**, where the subconscious thought process runs wild, and your mind makes connections more freely. Similar to how the brainstorming process allows for creative exploration and expression of all sources of inspiration, your mind stays open to all ideas (even the crazy ones). Taking a step away from the problem allows your brain to stay in this stage longer and facilitates the separation of bad ideas and maturation of good ones.

The third stage is **Illumination**, and it's often where the "eureka!" moment happens. Possible solutions are transferred from your subconscious to your conscious mind as a moment of insight, and endorphins kick in. Bringing this back to Sally's quote, I often describe this stage to my students as "the moment of idea conception:" All those sources of inspiration fighting with one another until one breaks through and fertilizes an idea.

Finally, you analyze and test those solutions during the **Verification** stage. Polish them to make sure they work and that they're valuable. If you start by asking the right questions and challenging assumptions early on to help you truly understand the problem, validating ideas should be a lot easier.

Finding your process

When looking at Wallas' four stages, it's easy to see something mystical in his hypothesis. He was a psychologist, after all. But his theories go a long way to prove that great ideas don't just come out of thin air.

Instead, great ideas tend to come out of other ideas. They're fueled by external stimuli that engage certain parts of the brain and fire off connections between the problem your mind is focused on and the potential solutions that are rattling around in there.

But what do you do when a creative block hits? Many prefer to walk through a museum when they feel depleted in inspiration. Some people's minds are more open when listening to music. Others while baking a cake, or swimming, or biking. French novelist Honoré de Balzac is rumored to have drunk 50 cups of coffee per day to stimulate his writing, and Russian composer Igor Stravinsky would do handstands to combat creative block.[50]

My personal "creative process" is heavily influenced by the media I'm ingesting at the time, so I'll take a break to read a collection of short stories or watch *Kung Fu Hustle* for the twenty-fifth time.[51] Anything to stimulate all the stuff that's floating around in my head.

I've found that, when all else fails, it can be equally stimulating just to get to work. Sometimes the solution lies in working through ideas—trying things out—to set yourself on the path to solid idea generation. A lot of that work will probably go in the trash, but that's ok. Remember: Ideas are disposable, so there's nothing wrong with committing brainpower to solutions that seem illogical (like a cross between a bear and a potato).

---

50. I don't recommend starting with this one.
51. Bill Murray said of *Kung Fu Hustle:* "There should have been a day of mourning for American comedy the day that movie came out."

Your process can only be your process. Just as a musician knows their instrument or an actor knows their method, practice and hard work are crucial to developing good habits.

The most important thing is that somewhere in that process lives rationale. Your inspirations don't have to be obvious, but your solutions do. All creative solutions must have value. Designers who post-rationalize decisions don't do anyone—themselves, the client, the brand—any good by tagging meaning or purpose onto a design at the end.

My best answer to the question posed at the beginning of this conversation is: Inspiration comes from everything, so feed your brain. As you'll learn in the next couple of conversations, your best ideas are apt to come from unlikely sources.

Bring your passions to work with you

Creative solutions often come from unlikely sources

I consider myself pretty old school when it comes to nerdery. I grew up with various 8- and 16-bit console controllers in my hands, but today prefer early coin-operated video games. My film vices pivot between 1970s kung fu and early spaghetti westerns, and I'll occasionally stay up until the small hours to catch Vincent Price or Hammer Films horror marathons.

My office shelves are littered with unread books—on topics ranging from 17th-century Dutch painting to the history of punctuation. I'm especially a sucker for anything from the Golden Age of science fiction through the New Wave era of the 1960s. This eclectic collection of material interests—in addition to being the source of so much of my entertainment—is the foundation of my internal ideation process; the way I make deep connections to solve complex problems.

After all, we are the sum total of our experiences, and those experiences equip us to tackle big, hairy problems.

Connecting experiences and finding a way to apply that resultant eureka effect to a current problem or practice—as we discussed in our last conversation—can be intensely gratifying. So let's explore that feeling. Here's what Golden Age science fiction and gestalt theory taught me about branding.

Making deep connections

A few years ago, I was working through The Library of America's two-volume *American Science Fiction: Nine Classic Novels of the 1950s.* Out of this selection from the Golden Age, I became particularly engrossed in Theodore Sturgeon's 1953 novel *More Than Human.* This story follows six unique individuals who can act as one conscious organism: A human gestalt.[52]

At the same time, I happened to be working on a comprehensive branding campaign for a new client. This tale I was reading of the next step in human evolution—what Sturgeon classifies as *homo gestalt*—made me realize that a company or product's brand works in much the same way as the novel's central characters. More specifically: *Should* work.

Like the characters of *More than Human,* brands are fully-functioning entities made up of individual parts. But designers often emphasize specific elements during the development process, like logos, which are often tasked with too much heavy lifting to carry a brand. They're

---

52. Sturgeon is also famous for inserting the line "live long and prosper" into an early *Star Trek* episode script.

usually one of the early visual components, but they don't have to be the cradle from which everything else is born.

Placing an equal amount of importance on all elements during the brand development process leads us to a more consistent, holistic approach to brand building that I began referring to as "gestalt branding."

Gestalt—translating to "shape" or "form" in German—refers to the inherent, guiding laws that allow us to recognize structure in elements *and* organize them into a perceived whole. Like how we tend to separate our fruits and vegetables into opposite drawers of the fridge or neatly arrange said fruits into a pleasing shape on the counter instead of randomly scattering them.

The central principle of gestalt is a two-way street, arguing that each "whole" can be deconstructed and perceived as its individual parts and vice versa.

Gestalt theories of perception are based on pure human nature: Our inclination to understand objects as an entire structure (the "whole") rather than the sum of its parts. A great example I've always used to detail this perception is the flashing lights of "electric tiara" marquees of 1930s movie theaters. Programmed with chase lighting—a series of adjacent light bulbs that cycle on and off frequently to give the illusion of lights moving along a path—our eyes interpret the consistent movement as if a single string of light is rapidly making its way around a rectangular track (the whole). But given enough reflection, our brain can pick apart this on/off pattern to understand the mechanics of the illusion (the individual parts).

Perception, order, meaning

When used together or independently in visual design, the gestalt laws of perception provide a framework for creating visual order. There are five, in particular, that warrant discussion:

The fundamental law of perception—**figure/ground**—relates to how the super team of eye and brain separate an object (figure) from its surroundings (ground). Reading this black text on a white background (flip that if you're in dark mode) easily explains how our eyes separate the two elements.

We naturally group by **similarity**. When items possess similar size, shape, color, or value, we move past individual identities in favor of a holistic understanding. A dozen geese become a gaggle, several hundred bees a swarm, and so on. We're naturally inclined to perceive group identities as stronger.[53]

The law of **proximity** describes how we perceive connections between elements, regardless of common traits. Designers utilize proximity to construct perceived relationships between different components. When multiple elements with common visual characteristics come together—through both similarity and proximity—unity occurs, and we perceive the larger organism rather than the individual parts (visualize a square made of 12 smaller squares).

Visual storytellers use the law of **continuation** to help the eye follow a particular path. On the low end, continuation can be understood as our eye following a continuous line or curve, and ignoring interruptions while seeking continued, implied shapes. A classic example is the Coca-Cola logo: Two separate words, each made of connected letters, with forms that flow from the first to the second. At a higher

---

53. Unless we're talking about the Beatles. Then it's John, Paul, George, and Ringo.

level, continuation is achieved in layout design to unite various elements, often by placing them along invisible grids that imply connectedness and provide our eye with a roadmap of reading order.

And finally, when the eye fills in missing information to form a complete shape, **closure** has occurred. Period. This one is pretty self-explanatory.

On their own, these individual principles provide context for a basic understanding of how we interpret visual clues and how designers use them to tell a story visually. It's when they intermingle and play well together—building layer upon layer of meaning—that things get interesting. Gestalt theory gives us insight into understanding and strengthening systems in a larger context.

Building brands that are more than human

So what exactly is this nonsense about gestalt branding surmised from a science fiction novel?

Reading about the interplay of characters—these individual elements working together to perform a higher function—I couldn't stop thinking about how multiple brand elements build a more extensive system. So I did a little research and found a 2009 study at the University of Notre Dame, which described the emotionally powerful brand of the American Girl doll as "the product of a complex system, or gestalt, whose component parts are in continuous interplay and together constitute a whole greater than their sum."

Aha! Proof that I'm not a crazy person.

As a longtime developer and manager of brand campaigns, I've always been fascinated by the ways that little experiences can make a big impact on how a company, or brand, is perceived. It's the whole of the cross-sensory experience that a brand offers—we're talking about everything from the emotion and the message to the way a brand personality literally feels, sounds, and smells—that leaves a lasting impression.

Like The Force, they're the elements that "surround and bind" it.[54]

Every well-developed brand has the potential to be a study in gestalt branding. From the color palette to the photography to the website, emails, and advertising campaign, individual pieces should work together to tell that brand's story, thus eliciting brand recognition. A pleasing experience for the customer that's more compelling than any individual marketing tactics could ever be.

Just like the homo gestalt of *More Than Human,* a strong conscience, or driving force, is needed to steer a brand in the right direction. This driving force (what we refer to as brand strategy) comprises research, statements (value proposition!), brand narrative, messaging matrices, etc., that we first spend time developing. It's what makes a brand work more than mere design, more than production.

Think of it like this: The act of assembling a skateboard from scratch is exciting, in addition to a literal exercise in gestalt processing. You start with a series of individual parts: Wheels, trucks, tape, and deck. When everything is assembled, you now have this new mode of transportation that takes on a whole new meaning and function. One that didn't exist before you unified those parts.

---

54. Sci-fi *and* film connection in one reference!

Now you begin to think of all the additional functions you can perform with that board: Grind some railings, shred an empty swimming pool. And your emotional connection to that skateboard continues to build. Eventually, you upgrade the wheels, slap on some stickers, and add plenty of battle scars from use.

All of that equity strengthens your ties to that board, and your connection to it moves from utility to love.

That's no different than how people interact with and perceive brands over time. Each impression, interaction, and new element adds to the overall interpretation; the perception of the whole.

When I was a full-time brand designer, these were the things that kept me too busy to chip away at my mountains of nerdery. Today, I'm still building that pile even higher and adding to my backlog of future experiences. And, frankly, I'm okay with that. Because when those future problems come along, I'll benefit from some new connection—some new thing I've learned—that will help me uniquely solve them. In a more than human way, you might say.

Keep everything in perspective

By focusing on one thing at a time

You can also connect your interests and experiences to form actionable ideas outside the problem-solving space. Sometimes, reflecting on a topic can help you learn something new about yourself, influence how you manage work, or even how you interact with other people.

In recent years, when thinking about the evolution of how I manage client relationships, I reflected on Deep Focus Cinematography. If you happen to be a student of film, you're likely familiar with the term as a hyperfocal technique made famous by director Orson Wells in *Citizen Kane* eighty-some years ago.

Essentially, a deep-focus shot includes foreground, middle-ground, and extreme-background objects, all in focus. By keeping multiple planes within the frame unified, Deep Focus is an approach that cinematographers use to create the impression of a fully realized, complex, layered world.

It's a tool that helps keep everything in perspective.

Once upon a time,[55] Deep Focus shots ruled the cinemas. Not only was everything sharp on screen, but the technique liberated the theater-goer's eye to have a broader view of the complete picture and a clear understanding of how every element contributed to the whole. As filmmakers drew their attention to the smaller television screen, the technique sadly faded.

Building relationships

As I've already mentioned a few times by now, I spent the first part of my design career working for creative agencies. Those familiar with this world understand it as a fast-paced environment that often prioritizes depth of capability—with little attention to individual client focus—and prides itself on fast delivery. Simply because deadlines often rule the agency-client relationship.

This hyper-focus on managing (often multiple) tight deadlines makes it nearly impossible to develop the complex, layered relationships that allow you to truly partner with your clients; to evolve together as partners.

That type of relationship building takes time, strategy, and diligence.

It wasn't until I switched to consulting that I realized the benefit of slowing down and focusing on one client at a time; investing yourself in ways that help build your partner's success, not just their brand.

---

55. Hey! Sergio Leone also famously used the Deep Focus technique in the opening scene of his masterpiece *Once Upon a Time in the West*.

This pivot allowed me to focus on all the unique aspects of relationship-building—like asking valuable questions and challenging existing assumptions—that can result in innovative and transformative outcomes for clients.

In all relationships, each project or effort starts at a different place on a continuum of growth and trust. Sometimes you're engaging with long-standing clients as a trusted partner, and other times you're beginning that relationship as a helping hand, concentrating on getting that first project to the finish line while planting those seeds of trust in your talents as an individual or as an organization.

However, you have the unique opportunity to drive toward bigger and better outcomes in both scenarios.

Taking a page from the early filmmakers I admire, I now employ a Deep Focus mindset to help me balance myself, my clients, my projects, and—most importantly—our results.

Staying focused

I talk to many people who pride themselves on their ability to multitask. I know I've done it myself; bragging about my ability to juggle many things at once. But being good at multitasking just means that you're good at doing many things poorly, simultaneously.

When your focus is too broad, it's easy to get mired down in these day-to-day tasks. Let's continue to use branding campaigns as an example. They often start with a long list of deliverables: A new logo, a website, and some marketing collateral. New uniforms for the guys in the factory would be nice. And, of course, we need to roll out new social marketing to tie into a wide-scale advertising campaign. And so forth.

Sure, you may need all of that stuff, *eventually.* But how are you supposed to stay focused on what's important when you already have a checklist that will keep creatives fighting to meet deadlines for the next nine months?

And we're just talking about one client here. If you're a freelancer or an art/creative director at an agency, you've probably got six more competing for your time and attention.

Deadline fatigue leads to less investment from both sides. And low investment leads to broken relationships. When you're an expert at what you do, the quality of attentive, hyper-focused relationships—rather than the quality of work—is often the catalyst that drives clients to check out what your competition is up to.

From people's individuality to the specific problems you're focused on solving, growth and evolution in relationship management and delivery happen when you focus on each part of your work, prioritizing the elements that drive the highest level of value for your clients. To successfully deliver all of the items on that list in a valuable way, you need to begin with strategy—period—before moving on to the next logical conversation.

Without a clear focus on where your client has been, where they are now, and where you're heading together, you can quickly lose sight of both sides' complete picture of success.

Strong relationships are built on individual people working together, performing a higher function to attain a common goal. Remember, design is a team sport. Staying focused on one aspect of the bigger picture at a time feeds into a complex system: A system of people, expertise, and values creating a solid conscience that helps steer everyone in the right direction.[56]

As home television screens get larger and resolution increases, there's no better time for a Deep Focus cinematography resurgence. Until that happens, think about how you can apply the concept to develop a better depth of field with your clients. Come up for air, consider your work in its totality, and evaluate how your daily work drives you and your partners toward success.

These are essential things to always keep in perspective.

---

56. Like Rocky Balboa said in *Creed:* "One step at a time. One punch at a time. One round at a time."

The future is human-centered

Supporting a people-first approach to solving problems

I obsessed over how things worked from a young age and often deconstructed my electronics: Computers, radios, watches... anything with intricate moving parts. As a kid, I spent countless summer hours at my grandmother's light fixture store, where I would wander the shop for things I could take apart or put together.

When I became more inquisitive, she would present me with boxes of loose parts and challenge me to make something with them. The terrifying thought of an unsupervised 10-year-old me experimenting with electricity aside; those challenges helped develop an inquisitive mindset that would only increase as time passed.

It's no surprise that I eventually found my way to an industry that places so much value on a curious mind.

Today, analyzing interactions, how things work, the steps it takes to accomplish something and questioning things that I find illogical or inefficient are natural aspects of who I am. Instead of wondering what the inside of a Walkman[57] looks like, I wonder, "how the hell does the Coke Freestyle machine keep my root beer from tasting like orange soda?"

I've learned that the answers to these kinds of questions are usually just a few simple conversations away.

Empathy leads to insights

Outside of this book, I spend a lot of time thinking, talking, and writing about how much I love the analytical, problem-solving culture of user experience (UX) research and design—the industry I landed in after nearly a decade of navigating the agency world. Through all of these efforts, there's one question I regularly get from both seasoned designers and students alike: "How do I get into user experience design?"

The career branding soldiers often worry that it's too late for such a "drastic" career shift.[58] At the same time, the soon-to-be-graduates feel ill-prepared to translate their graphic design education to a field that's rarely discussed during their coursework; unable to see how they can apply the fundamentals of graphic design to a (mostly) digital field.

Another, more unfortunate, aspect at play here is the assumption that designing websites and apps also means building websites and apps. That's a falsehood perpetuated by way too many university programs pairing coding and design together.

I can't recount how many times I've heard, "I'd love to design a website, but I don't know how to code." That hurts my design-loving

---

57. Consider this the grandfather of the iPod, if you even remember what an iPod was.
58. I've been there as well, and I get it.

heart. A good understanding of both disciplines and how they work together is a massive plus in this world. But we're talking about two very different toolsets here, each requiring its own mastery.

Over time I've been able to pair my response down to a pretty simple answer, on the surface: User experience design is less about what you know than it is about what you value. It's less about your design chops than it is about how your brain works.

And then comes the curveball: You don't even need to be good at design to be great at user experience design. If you happen to find yourself at this same turning point in your career, the real question you need to ask is: "Is user experience right for me?"

If you've ever had a conversation with a user experience designer or researcher, you probably heard them talk about empathy. A lot. It's a true—but often overused—concept we rely on to explain our prime directive. But it goes way beyond just "caring."

UX design is a broad, cross-disciplinary field where design and research go hand in hand, so we constantly learn and apply new techniques and try on new hats. We balance strong communication skills with meaningful listening skills, and synthesize our findings with analytical problem-solving skills.

We all come from wildly diverse backgrounds. Sure, many of us are well-versed in most creative fields and strategy techniques. And because UX is still an emerging industry, many of us got our start in the graphic design world. But not as many as you think.

Some of us design, some research, and many do a little of both. The experience design field is also full of creative and ambitious writers, thinkers, and tinkerers passionate about listening to what people want and uncovering human-centered solutions.

To excel at user experience, you have to really value human relationships and do so through an empathetic lens (there I go with the "empathy" thing). It doesn't matter if we're talking about human relationships with technology, physical experiences, or other people: We just want those relationships and interactions to be more enjoyable. Or more meaningful. Or more productive. You get the idea.

We do this by relying on a human-focused strategy to deepen relationships and increase loyalty through an empathetic, people-first approach called Human-Centered Design. Because we believe that observing and listening to people leads to better business decisions and more meaningful experiences.

Solving real problems for real people

Human-Centered Design is a framework for solving problems that involves the human perspective every step of the way. It's an approach driven by the needs and motivations of the people who will use the products or services; not clients, not businesses.

Following a human-centered approach is especially valuable for keeping clients focused on the big picture—and strategic outcomes— of any effort. Because it's so often easy for them to forget they (likely) aren't the target audience for their product or experience.

As human-centered problem solvers, our job is often to translate business value into user value. Focusing not on what we want or what the client wants, but what the user wants. Empathizing with the end-user—keeping their needs and desires at the forefront of all decisions—is the key to designing products and experiences that people will use and love.[59]

---

59. Collaboration skills are also a plus. Successful design solutions don't manifest in silos.

Albert Einstein said, "The important thing is not to stop questioning; curiosity has its own reason for existing." Rightfully so, the possession of an infinitely curious mind is a huge plus in this industry. When solving real-world problems for real people, a curious, question-based approach never fails to support informed decisions, and keeps you focused on your actual client: The user.[60]

You might be thinking, "where does design fit into all of this?" We often conduct interviews that lead to persona and journey map creation to generate this understanding. Those behavioral observations may involve low-fi wireframes, with outcomes leading to high-fidelity prototypes. And then? We take those prototypes and talk to those people some more, further validating and iterating until we reach a solution that most effectively serves them.

All of that is design work, too. Design isn't just about colors and screens; it's about people, and processes, and technology, and on and on.

Regardless of the approach, or tools used, the primary goal is to fully understand a person's pains so that we can better address their needs before the "traditional" design work happens.[61]

So if you're the type of person that wants to build a more empathetic and well-designed world that works better for everyone, then the user experience field is probably right for you. If you're less interested in capturing new customers and more focused on helping businesses retain the ones they already have—while also making them happier—then ditto.

---

60. I'll cover how to do this in the next conversation.
61. I guarantee there's no right or wrong process.

And making that jump from the agency world, or straight out of design school, won't be as difficult as you expected as long as you've got the right mindset.

Most of us came to this field because of our passions and motivations, not necessarily our design background. You may see a transition to the still-emerging UX design field as an evolution—or the logical next step in your career—fueled by the allure of bigger, sexier work. And you wouldn't necessarily be wrong.

However, if you believe that humans should live at the center of every design decision, if you enjoy solving big hairy problems, and if you're interested in more meaningful work that improves other people's lives, then UX design is something you should strongly consider. Because the future of design is human-centered.

Now let's learn how to put that empathetic, curious mind into practice.

Be a learner, not a knower

How asking the right questions leads to better solutions

Do you ever think about the play icon? It's pretty... iconic. At a glance, an incredibly high percentage of people are likely to understand, instantly, what it's communicating and how to interact with it. That's an example of what The Father of UX, Don Norman, would refer to as an affordance: An existing relationship between an object and a person that implies an expected outcome.[62]

Regardless of the interface—YouTube, Netflix, or even a VCR—we're reasonably confident we know how to initiate a video when we come across a small, right-facing triangle.

Growing up with the everyone-has-a-microwave-in-the-home generation, it's a symbol I've never questioned. A friend of mine argues that we—those early tech crash test dummies—learned the ins and

---

62. Norman published the seminal work *The Design of Everyday Things* in 1988. You should read it.

outs of technology through ignorant fearlessness. We learned how to operate the VCR because we were naive enough to push all the buttons and wait for a response.

We also had way more buttons in those days (and more questions).

Today, rather than poking around on my own, I learn from asking those questions; obsessing over how things work by analyzing interactions. It's an exercise that often relies on flat-out talking to people. Every time you question how things work, you collect data on everyday interactions and strengthen your understanding of what works and why people love "this thing" versus "that thing."

When I lived in the marketing with a big M world, we often talked about knowing our audience. It's where I learned to associate "knowing" with top-level data such as unique monthly site visitors, conversion rates, and other general analytics. But while all of that data is measurable, it doesn't give you the metrics you need to understand what people think or how they act.

You see, "knowing" can't always be trusted, as the concept itself leads to more questions. "Understanding," instead, is about getting into the hearts and minds of the people behind those numbers so you can make more informed decisions. Knowing allows you to target a specific type of person, while understanding provides a path to designing loveable products and experiences.

"We know" is a phrase that often leads to failure. And we all fail at following our own advice sometimes.

I don't understand

A few years ago, my mom agreed to watch our kids at our home so that my wife and I could go out. The kids wanted to watch a movie later that night, so to help her out, I got everything set up, handed her the remote, and told her to "just hit play" whenever they were ready.

And she said, "Which button is that?"

I was shocked, so after a pause, I answered, "...The play button."

And she repeated her question.

Now, when it comes to my interactions with my mother, I'm the type of person that will pick my hill and die on it, so, of course, I answered again with, "The play button." But I put a little more emphasis on it this time, hoping that would clear things up.

She responded that she didn't know which button I was talking about, so I kind of pumped my fists and emphatically stated: "The play button! This is a universally-understood symbol with 30+ years of history behind it." Then I graciously pointed at the button.

And she said, "Well, you should have just said 'push the arrow.'"[63]

Come to find out, my mom—65 years old at the time of this event—never used a remote in her life. At home, she still got up and walked to the TV to change the channel, turn it on/off, adjust the volume, etc. Though I was surprised by this revelation, I realized that I got caught up in the expectation that we shared a similar understanding. I should have asked questions rather than knowing *I was right* and assuming *she misunderstood.*

The learner mindset

When we treat our views as objective facts, it's easy to make mistakes

---

63. This, of course, led to another conversation about the function of arrow buttons on a remote.

driven by assumptions. In the case of Jon v. Mom, the stakes were minimal. But when a company or brand fails to seek understanding, the consequences could be ruinous.

Take the story of the dairy substitute brand Silk, for example. Silk's big break came in 1978 when a national supermarket chain started carrying its products. Today, most of us know that soy milk, almond milk, and the like are shelf-stable, meaning they don't have to be refrigerated until open. But initially, Silk products were parked in the produce section, next to fresh fruits and nuts.

That placement made sense to the makers of Silk, but in the late 1970s, few consumers were willing to give warm "milk" a try. Silk was making some brash assumptions in their attempt to disrupt a pretty stable market without so much as talking to consumers.

Unsurprisingly, sales were consistently low until someone had the genius idea to move Silk products to the refrigerated case next to the dairy milk. This simple move—of catering to consumers' expectations—not only saved their brand but put the product in a competitive (and expected) space.

In 1978 the makers of Silk knew their product, but they didn't *understand* their customers because they didn't talk to them. Forty years later, non-dairy milk represents nearly 20% of the overall dairy market.

Experience = understanding

After working in the agency world for many years, I found that I was being discouraged from asking questions more and more often. Usually, ones that I felt were critical to understanding the goals of a project or necessary for reacting to client feedback. The need to make the client happy often prevented really valuable conversations from taking place.

It's through those honest, face-to-face conversations that real problems are often solved. A defining example being the story—more likely legend—of Betty Crocker cake mix.

In the 1950s, General Mills launched Betty Crocker cake mix in a box. By formulating a complete recipe made of dry goods, General Mills birthed—what they thought to be—a revolutionary product in the early days of American consumerism: All the ingredients of a cake; just add water.

The product was marketed as an error-free alternative for busy homemakers, saving both time and effort to make way for other household duties.

But it didn't sell well.

So they decided to talk to their audience and found that the average American housewife felt terrible about using the product. The cakes were great, but the credit they got from their friends and family felt way more than they deserved. The product actually made users feel deceitful. So they gave up.

Instead of coming up with a slick advertising campaign telling the modern housewife (remember, this was the 1950s) that it was ok to have more time for laundry, cleaning, and other household chores, General Mills altered the product to require the addition of a fresh egg to the mix.

This small change of adding a fresh ingredient to the process made consumers feel less guilt about using the product, and today people rarely bake a cake from "scratch."

The lesson we learn from this story—true or untrue—is that we often need to experience the pain first to understand it. Approaching problems with ignorance and a curious mind allows you to dig beneath the surface of those problems by asking questions and placing assumptions aside. That's how you learn to empathize; to understand how people think and act. And empathy leads to better solutions designed for real people.

It's important to remember that we don't always embrace things just because they simplify our lives.

There's no need to reinvent the wheel (or knob)

In product design, we often benefit from sticking to expectations for interface and functionality to build products that work the way people expect. Before reinventing the wheel, before trying to innovate, one must first understand the value—the time, effort, and knowledge—that went into the thing they are attempting to disrupt.

The first car radio, released in 1930, had a rotating knob that adjusted the volume up by turning it to the right and down by turning it to the left. And 90 years later, we're still using radio knobs the same way.

When people already understand a format, why force them to learn something new?

But 2016 saw the launch of a Honda Pilot crossover that did away with the standard volume knob in favor of a volume control slider; a feature on the vehicle's touchscreen interface. By 2019, the old-fashioned knob was back due to numerous consumer complaints.

If Honda product designers had asked users about their typical interactions with a volume knob, they would have found that we reach for it to turn the music down when we're having a conversation or listening to navigation. Or quickly turn it up when we hear our favorite song or the cheer of a crowd during a baseball game broadcast. It's a tool that provides quick results without taking our attention from the road.

It's more familiar to us than steering wheel controls or voice-activated features and, therefore, our most reliable volume control when driving an unfamiliar vehicle with an unfamiliar dashboard.

Implementing features that require precise hand interactions and taking drivers' eyes off the road for an extended time is a reckless use of technology. In an attempt to "modernize" their vehicle's interface, Honda disrupted a lifetime of driving habits. That's a big gamble on technology.

The Honda story teaches us that more technology isn't always the answer, and reinforces the idea that affordances (and familiarity) drive usability.

Together, these stories teach us that innovation doesn't come without insight. You have to know how people think and feel to truly validate ideas. Surveys and focus groups can be soulless and impersonal, but conversations between people align understanding and foster honest communication. It's said that Henry Ford famously stated, "If I had asked people what they wanted, they would have said faster horses," when implying that innovation can happen without consumer input. While there's no actual proof he said it, the concept may have worked in the 1920s. But in today's everyone-is-a-user marketplace, people are more likely just to tap "skip survey."

Epilogue

Keep failing forward

A couple of years ago, I taught an online design portfolio course for soon-to-be graduates. Many students had received the same foundational design education, but all had different strengths and interests they hoped to pursue after college. So I decided to supplement that semester's course load by hosting conversations with people I know in the industry—touching as many corners of the design world as possible. I brought in experts in everything from motion design to branding, illustration to product design, and so forth.

During one of these weekly conversations, a former colleague told my students, "I wish I could return to my college career and learn from Jon. He has a lot of experience in many areas that he's open about regarding what he did wrong and what he did right. He's made as many or more mistakes in his career as he's had successes."

I'd never thought of it that way. On the one hand, it felt like high praise. On the other, I was intrigued by the idea that learning from mistakes leads to growth. Exploring this concept and reflecting on all the things I'd done right—and wrong—was a massive push for me to write this book.

Whether you're still a student or have been navigating the design world for 20+ years like myself, we're all where we are today because we tried some things and either figured it out or didn't. But should we really be proud of our mistakes? Hell yes! Just as much, or more so, as our successes.

Why? Because putting yourself on a path to failure means you've got courage. You can't be afraid to fail because failure is a great teacher.

However, you have to learn to trust yourself first to fail successfully. To understand the power that lives in your thoughts, ideas, and expertise because they're uniquely yours. Everyone is making things up as they go.

This book has been about how I did it. How are you going to fail, and learn, and succeed?

The design industry is ever-evolving. Versatile, T-shaped people are in more demand due to their ability to collaborate across disciplines, build high-performing relationships, and foster innovation. The creative problem solvers of the future will be able to navigate through ambiguity and uncertainty; have a sensitivity and empathy for people; and understand varied methods for framing problems, generating ideas, and validating solutions.

You don't need a perfect portfolio, a specific degree, or even a fancy title to prove that you're capable of continued success in the changing design climate. You just need to have an appetite for risk and a curious mind. You need to be comfortable with getting uncomfortable about pushing the boundaries of your skills in—and understanding of—design.[64]

---

64. In his speech known as "We Choose to go to the Moon," John F. Kennedy said we choose to do these things "not because they are easy, but because they are hard... because that challenge is one that we are willing to accept, one we are unwilling to postpone." This,

And if your face doesn't light up when you talk about it, you may want to look for a new career.

All of your design knowledge is valuable and deserves a forum. Meaning that whether you like it or not, you're capable of teaching too. So you should talk to people about design. Write about it. Work up the courage to stand in front of an audience and share something you've learned or the mistakes you've made, and people will listen.

Sure, it may be advice or learnings they've heard before, but they haven't heard it from *you.*

I want to leave you with this last piece of advice: There's little room for ego in this industry. Fail fast, do it with grace, and keep moving. Designers that become reliant only on the knowledge they already possess, *too complacent with the way they work*, or too married to their ideas—and are afraid to let it all burn when needed—are destined to atrophy.

Design is an industry of many colors, not black and white. So keep evolving. Keep learning. And embrace all failures as a step toward something better.

---

too, is a choice. Not an easy one, but a valuable one.

Recommended reading

People always say that books are authored on the backs of other books. And they're correct for saying that. Everything on this list expands on topics covered in this book, impacted how I approach my job, or can help you think differently about how you do yours. There are also a few things that I just don't want to see lost to time.

I'm always looking for a good book recommendation, so find me online and give me yours.

Articulating Design Decisions: Communicate with Stakeholders, Keep Your Sanity, and Deliver the Best User Experience (2nd Edition)

Tom Greever, 2020

Tom managed to write a whole book about a topic I covered in just a few pages. It's an excellent resource for anyone struggling to explain the intent behind their design decisions; for newbies and managers alike. This book is a must-read if you work with clients, business partners, or product stakeholders.

Bluebeard: A Novel

Kurt Vonnegut, 1987

Because I love Vonnegut. Bluebeard is a lesser-known but equally strong entry from his catalog. Plus, I wanted to provide an opposing perspective. You just spent several hours of your life burning any remains of your artist identity, so why not spend an equal amount of time in the mind of an artist? This book stacks up with some of the great portraits of fictional artists, like W. Somerset Maugham's *The Moon and Sixpence* and Chaim Potok's *My Name is Asher Lev.* You should be able to find them all in your local library.

Damn Good Advice (For People with Talent!): How To Unleash Your Creative Potential by America's Master Communicator
George Lois, 2012

A lifetime of advice from the man the *Wall Street Journal* called "prodigy, *enfant terrible,* founder of agencies, creator of legends." I tend to gift copies of this book to the designers I manage and almost always screen his remarkable TED talk "If you do it right, it, and you, will live forever" with my students.

Design is Storytelling and Graphic Design Thinking: Beyond Brainstorming
Ellen Lupton, 2017 and 2011

I lumped these together since they're from the same author. Most of Lupton's books center on aesthetics, praising the output of design as a product of creativity. Not these two! *Design is Storytelling* will help you bring the narrative power of your work to life, and *Graphic Design Thinking* is all about process and research. And in true Lupton fashion, both books are beautiful.

Don't Make Me Think, Revisited: A Common Sense Approach to Web and Mobile Usability (3rd Edition)

Steve Krug, 2014

The world is full of poor design; full of confusing or complicated to use products. Products that make us think too hard about the goals we're trying to accomplish. This book will teach you how to eliminate those question marks. Krug laid out many valuable—and simple—principles on human-computer interaction that, 20 years after the first edition, are still very relevant for anyone designing experiences today.

Feck Perfuction: Dangerous Ideas on the Business of Life

James Victore, 2019

Victore is one of the few remaining artists in the design world. This book is mainly written for the practicing "creative genius" and artist and is full of brutal honesty about design, art, humor, knowing thyself, and embracing authenticity. Plus his signature mustache.

The Hucksters

Frederic Wakeman, 1945

A portrait of the emerging Post-World War II advertising world, before Madison Avenue was the center of it and radio still ruled. If you're interested in reading about the birth of modern design, then go hunt for a used copy of this novel. The narration of a train ride from New York to Hollywood is worth it alone.

It Doesn't Have to Be Crazy at Work

Jason Fried and David Heinemeier Hansson, 2018

Fried and Hansson write, "It's time to stop celebrating Crazy, and start celebrating Calm." This glimpse into the culture at 37Signals/Basecamp had as big of an impact on the way I view my workdays (and workplace) as *Sprint* from the Google Ventures team. The authors provide a fresh perspective on the modern workplace, and you'll find yourself agreeing with almost every declarative.

The Process is the Inspiration

House Industries, 2017

A whole coffee table book dedicated to the question: "Where do you find inspiration?" The people at House Industries expound on process, obsessive curiosity, and bringing your passions to work way better than I ever could.

User Friendly: How the Hidden Rules of Design Are Changing the Way We Live, Work, and Play

Cliff Kuang and Robert Fabricant, 2020

The authors "reveal the untold story of a paradigm that quietly rules our modern lives: The assumption that machines should anticipate what we need." *User Friendly* is essential reading if you care about user-friendly design. After a dozen or so pages, you'll reconsider your relationship with technology.

Index

Thank you

First, thank you for caring enough about design to pick this book up. It doesn't matter if you pre-ordered it, received it as a gift, borrowed it from a friend, checked it out from your library, or found it in a bargain bin at a used bookstore. I hope you learned something. I hope you highlighted the hell out of it. I left plenty of room in the margins, so I hope you scribbled in your own thoughts, stories, and ideas to make it better, like the spell book from that Harry Potter movie I can't remember the name of. I want to challenge you to pass it on to someone else so they can do the same.

Thank you to my wife, Justine, for reading every word and prompting me to clarify so many passages for others who, like her, don't speak design. And to my kids for giving me precious moments of time to write this.

Thank you to James Campbell and Jake Heberlie, the first "bosses" I had that would feel really uncomfortable about me calling them my boss. And to Jeremy Huggins for encouraging me to start writing again several years ago and always giving me the honest, critical feedback I need that others would be reluctant to give.

Thank you to Billy Frazier, Danny Harms, and Laura and Jacob White for proofreading early drafts to help me find focus and remind me what I was trying to say.

I probably wouldn't have started this effort without the people who took the time to have virtual conversations with me when the world needed to be apart and reminded me how important it is for us to stay connected and share knowledge for the sake of sanity, and humanity.

So thank you to all the people I've managed and coached over the years for listening to this advice time and again and never telling me to shut up, all my former students who probably wanted to, and everyone in my design network for the "yes, and" attitude that helped shape so much of this.

Finally, thank you to all of my current and former co-workers and collaborators who taught me the power of people working together and sharing ideas.

Colophon

This book is set in Vollkorn (pronounced *Follkorn*), the first typeface designed by Friedrich Althausen, who began developing the letterforms while studying at the Bauhaus in Weimar, Germany. A Renaissance period-inspired variable font, Vollkorn has been described as having "dark and meaty serifs and a bouncing and healthy look." In German, the typeface's name translates to *wholemeal,* referring to the small everyday-use fonts from the days of handset type. Vollkorn is free to use—available under the Open Font License—and you can donate to the project at vollkorn-typeface.com.

About
the author

Jon Robinson is not an artist. He's currently the Director of Product Design for an east coast-based, virtual healthcare company. Before

that, he freelanced, worked for creative agencies, spent time at small not-for-profits and on in-house design teams, and built experiences for global brands as an experience strategy and design consultant. Jon has a bachelor's degree in art history and graphic design from Illinois Wesleyan University and graduate degrees in creative technologies, from Illinois State University, and design thinking, from Indiana University.

At heart, he's a polymath. In spirit, he's someone who would never actually use the word "polymath." He's lectured and spoke on everything from user experience to the convenience economy, from service design to his passion for anything published by Kurt Vonnegut. He's available to speak at your conference or attend your trivia event, as long as there's an open bar.

In addition to his general love for learning, Jon taught design for nearly a decade: Most recently with the School of Art, Design, and Media at Lindenwood University and the Sam Fox School of Design & Visual Arts at Washington University in St. Louis. He was previously a co-author of *97 Things Every UX Practitioner Should Know* from O'Reilly Media. Jon lives with his wife and two children in Missouri.